The Community
of the Book

The Community of the Book

A Directory of Selected Organizations and Programs

Compiled by Carren O. Kaston

Edited and with an Introduction by
John Y. Cole
Executive Director, The Center for the Book

Transaction Books
New Brunswick (U.S.A.) and Oxford (U.K.)

Copyright © 1987 by Transaction, Inc.
New Brunswick, New Jersey 08903

All rights reserved under International and Pan-American Copyright Conventions. No part of this book may be reproduced or transmitted in any form or by any means, electronic or mechanical, including photocopy, recording, or any information storage and retrieval system, without prior permission in writing from the publisher. All inquiries should be addressed to Transaction Books, Rutgers—The State University, New Brunswick, New Jersey 08903.

Library of Congress Catalog Number: 86-600010
ISBN: 0-88738-145-6
Printed in the United States of America

Library of Congress Cataloging in Publication Data

Kaston, Carren, 1946–
  The Community of the book.

  Bibliography: p.
  Includes index.
  1. Bibliography societies—Directories. 2. Books
and reading—United States—Societies, etc.—Directories.
3. Book industries and trade—United States—Societies,
etc.—Directories. 4. Literacy—United States—Societies,
etc.—Directories. 5. Book and reading—Societies, etc.
—Directories. 6. Book industries and trade—Societies,
etc.—Directories. 7. Literacy—Societies, etc.—Directories. I. Cole, John Young, 1940– . II. Center for
the Book. III. Title.
Z1008.K38 1986   002′.06073   86-600010

ISBN 0-88738-145-6

Contents

Preface

This is a selective listing of organizations that promote books and reading, administer literacy projects, and encourage the study of books. Expanding on the brief list of organizations in the 1984 Library of Congress report, *Books in Our Future,* it focuses on national programs of special interest to the Center for the Book in the Library of Congress. We hope, however, that it will also be useful to the entire book community. The emphasis is on organizations in the United States, where recently there has been renewed interest in educational reform, in literacy, and in the "future of the book." International book programs, while included, have been described in greater detail in two other publications available from the Center for the Book: *U.S. International Book Programs 1981* (1982) and *U.S. Books Abroad: Neglected Ambassadors,* by Curtis G. Benjamin (1984).

The Center for the Book in the Library of Congress is a national catalyst for stimulating public interest in books and reading and for encouraging the study of books and the printed word. Its symposia and projects, including this publication, are made possible by private contributions from individuals and corporations. Special thanks for this project go to compiler Carren Kaston, to Linda Cox, who prepared the manuscript for publication, and to Joseph Brinley, who provided valuable editorial help and prepared the index.

John Y. Cole
Executive Director
The Center for the Book
November 1985

Is There a Community of the Book?

An Introduction

John Y. Cole

Is there a "community of the book?" The Center for the Book in the Library of Congress was established in 1977 on the assumption that such a community exists and that it can be mobilized to keep books and reading central in our lives and in the life of our democracy. A partnership between the Library of Congress and private citizens and organizations, the Center for the Book is a national catalyst for stimulating public interest in books and reading and for encouraging the study of books and the printed word.

The most important person in this partnership or community is the individual reader. Librarian of Congress Daniel J. Boorstin, the center's founder, made this clear when the center was created, saying, "As the national library of a great free republic, the Library of Congress has a special duty and a special interest to see that books do not go unread...here we shape plans for a grand national effort to make all our people eager, avid, understanding, critical readers."[1] In *A Nation of Readers,* a talk he presented in 1982, Boorstin asserted that our country was built on books and reading and that, at least in the past, America has been a nation of readers.[2] We can be so again, he maintains, if our citizens and institutions make a new commitment to keeping "the Culture of the Book" thriving.[3] In this effort, which is the basic mission of the Center for the Book, technology is an ally: "We have a special duty to see that the book is the useful, illuminating servant of all other technologies, and that all other technologies become the effective, illuminating acolytes of the book."[4]

Publisher Samuel S. Vaughan, in his essay "The Community of the Book" in the Writer 1983 issue of *Daedalus,* defines the book community as one that "consists of those for whom the written word, especially as expressed in printed and bound volumes, is of the first importance." Its major inhabitants are authors, editors, publishers, booksellers, librarians, wholesalers, literary agents and literary critics, book reviewers and book journalists, translators, educators, and "not least, though often omitted from full partnership— readers." In iconoclastic fashion, Vaughan challenges many common assertions about books and publishing. By the time he is finished, he also challenges his own basic assumption:

> It is convenient to think of ourselves as the Community of the Book. But perhaps we are destined to remain a series of separate states, warring factions, shouting imprecations at each other across borders....I hope not. For we are bound up in common concerns and causes; we do need each other, and for the usual reasons—because we are mutually dependent.[5]

The search for a "book community" in the United States is not new. The story before the founding of the Center for the Book is a mixture of solid accomplishments and periods of frustration, which reflect both the tenuous nature of alliances among book-minded people and traditional American uncertainty about the proper role of government in culture, education, and the world of books.[6]

In 1950 a small group of leading American publishers, including Cass Canfield of Harper & Row, Curtis McGraw from McGraw-Hill, Harold Guinzburg of Viking Press, and Douglas Black of Doubleday and Company, established the American Book Publishers Council (ABPC), a trade association that would extend itself beyond usual business concerns in order to promote books, reading, and libraries. The first discussions between ABPC representatives and librarians took place at the 1950 annual conference of the American Library Association (ALA). Postal rates, book distribution, copyright, and reading promotion were early agenda items.[7] The anthology *The Wonderful World of Books* (1952) was a result of the 1951 Conference on Rural Reading, sponsored by the ABPC, the U.S. Department of Agriculture, the ALA, and other organizations. Theodore Waller, the first managing director (1950-53) of the ABPC, and Dan Lacy, who succeeded Waller and guided the ABPC's affairs until he joined McGraw-Hill in 1966, were the key figures in forging these early book world alliances.

Censorship became a topic of mutual concern to publishers and librarians in the early 1950s, when private groups and public officials in various parts of the country made attempts to remove books from sale, to censor textbooks, to distribute lists of "objectionable" books or authors, and to purge libraries. Senator Joseph R. McCarthy's Senate Subcommittee on Investigations, for example, demanded that the overseas information libraries of the State Department be purged of books that presented "pro-Communist" views. In response, in May 1953 the ALA and the ABPC sponsored a conference on the Freedom to Read. Librarian of Congress Luther H. Evans chaired the two-day meeting, which resulted in substantial agreement on principles and soon led to a Freedom to Read Declaration that was adopted by both associations. The American Booksellers Association, the Book Manufacturers' Institute, the National Council of Teachers of English, and other groups soon added their endorsements.

The Freedom to Read Declaration and related intellectual freedom issues united publishing and library leaders and their organizations and stimulated, in 1954, the creation of the National Book Committee. Declaring itself a citizen-oriented, public interest voice on behalf of books, the book committee urged the "wider distribution and wider use" of books and encouraged greater use and support of libraries, the development of lifelong reading habits, improved access to books, and the freedom to read. Its approximately three hundred members worked together and with the professional book community to "foster a general public understanding of the value of books to the individual and to a democratic society."

The American Book Publishers Council and the American Library Association, the primary sponsors of the National Book Committee, provided the committee with its small (but paid) professional staff and office space. Most of its projects were supported by grants from foundations or by government funds. A Commission on the Freedom to Read was established in 1955. In 1958 the book committee inaugurated National Library Week, a year-round promotion and media campaign that encouraged citizen support for libraries, which it administered in collaboration with the ALA for the next sixteen years. In 1960 the committee began administering the National Book Awards. For the next decade it initiated and cosponsored, with a wide variety of organizations, useful conferences on topics such as the development of lifelong reading habits, the role of U.S. books abroad, books in the schools, the need for books in rural areas as well as in urban slums, the need to strengthen school libraries, and the public library in the city. The book committee also guided development of a "Reading Out Loud" educational television series, which was produced by the Westinghouse Broadcasting Company, and sponsored the initial publication of enduring classics such as Nancy Larrick's *Parent's Guide to Children's Reading* and G. Robert Carlsen's *Books and the Teen-Age Reader.*[8]

The National Book Committee's sponsorship of projects and publications about the role of American books overseas, particularly in Asia and Africa, reflected widespread recognition of the key role that books could play in economic and cultural development. American government officials, publishers, educators, and librarians established several important programs that stimulated book exports, foreign trade, and international exchange; encouraged publishing in developing countries; and promoted books, libraries, and reading around the world. The major programs were the Informational Media Guaranty Program (IMG) (1948-68), a program which borrowed funds from the U.S. Treasury to enable United States book publishers, as well as producers of other "informational media" such as films and recordings, to sell their materials in countries that were short of hard-currency foreign exchange; Franklin Book Programs, Inc. (1952-79), a nonprofit, private educational corporation initiated by the publishing community and supported by U.S. government information agencies and foundations to "assist developing countries in the creation, production, distribution, and use of books and other educational materials"; and the Government Advisory Committee on Book and Library Programs (1962-77), a panel of publishers, booksellers, and librarians that met with government officials to provide advice about federal book policies and programs.[9]

Unesco proclaimed the year 1972 as International Book Year in order to "focus the attention of the general public (and of) governments and international and domestic organizations on the role of books and related materials in the lives and affairs of the individual and society." The National Book Committee organized and supported U.S. participation in International Book Year. The year 1972 was, in retrospect, a high watermark in the United States for cooperative organizational efforts on behalf of books and reading. Two years later the National Book Committee itself was disbanded, in 1977 the Government Advisory Committee on Book and Library Programs was abolished, and in 1979 Franklin Book Programs was formally liquidated. So in 1982, when Unesco sponsored a World Congress on Books to assess international progress in promoting books since 1972, several of the key United States organizations that had participated in International Book Year were gone.

What had happened to the programs that made the 1960s and early 1970s such a productive period of cooperation in the United States book community? The Informational Media Guaranty Program was terminated in 1968 when the U.S. Congress, concerned about the large indebtedness to the U.S. Treasury incurred by the IMG program, denied funds to the United States Information Agency for the program's administration. According to publisher Curtis G. Benjamin, this final controversy over the method of funding IMG was only one of a long series of misunderstandings: "to some [IMG] was a government propaganda device, to others it was a subsidy of commercial exporters, and to still others it spelled censorship." Benjamin, writing in 1984, expressed his hope "that a new (and much simplified) IMG-type program will somehow and soon be organized to meet the challenges that are today as critical as they were in the last decades following World War II."[10]

The National Book Committee was formally dissolved on November 15, 1974. Several related problems had become insurmountable. These included inflationary increases in costs, drastically lessened support from the publishing industry, and the committee's inability to raise basic operating funds from sources outside publishing. In December 1972, the committee had lost the funding and support through services in kind it previously had received from the Association of American Publishers (the successor to the American Book Publishers Council); this separation, according to John C. Frantz, the book committee's former executive director, "came at the worst time in the Book Committee's financial affairs." Other problems also plagued the committee, including management difficulties and disagreements among publishers and librarians about the administration of major projects such as the National Book Awards. A fundamental fund-raising difficulty, according to Frantz, was the committee's inability "to overcome its apparently incompatible, not to say schizoid, origins" and reach far enough beyond the library and publishing professions "to achieve a separate, clearly defined identity."[11] In a parting tribute that called attention to "the many fine things" that had happened to books and reading because of the National Book Committee, the editors of *Publishers Weekly* ruefully noted that "some day it will have to be reinvented."[12]

The Government Advisory Committee on Book and Library Programs not only had advisory and review functions but also was a valuable forum for discussing programs of mutual concern to the government and the private sector, for example, international copyright, tariffs on educational books, and overseas distribution of American scientific books. It also supported Unesco initiatives such as the International Book Year. In 1977, however, President Jimmy Carter asked that all "nonessential" government advisory groups be abolished. The State Department, citing the reduced role that books and libraries by then were playing in the programs of the United States Information Agency and the U.S. Agency for International Development and noting an increased private sector role in international book activity, recommended that the advisory committee be terminated. This recommendation was accepted in April 1977, and the committee was abolished.

By 1977 Franklin Book Programs, Inc., a significant venture in international publishing that used government and private funds, was also struggling for existence. The major reason was rapidly decreasing support from the United States Information Agency, which had helped fund Franklin from its beginning, but Franklin also faced internal financial and management difficulties, particularly in certain field offices. The United States Information Agency had also become increasingly particular about which publications it would subsidize, causing controversy and ill will between Franklin representatives and government officials. According to Curtis G. Benjamin, Franklin Books forfeited much of its U.S. government support by "refusing to limit its sponsorship to books that were strictly in line with U.S. foreign policy objectives as interpreted by U.S. Information Agency program officers."[13] Franklin had financed its operating costs by its own earnings and by contributions from United States foundations, corporations, and individuals through overhead allowances from grants and contracts. With government and foundation interest in its activities sharply decreased, in October 1977 Franklin Book's board of directors suspended all operations. The decision to close the corporation came the next year and liquidation was completed in 1979. Franklin's remaining cash balance and receivables, amounting to less than $10,000, were contributed to the Center for the Book in the Library of Congress.

Leadership changes in publishing and librarianship in the 1960s were one reason why cooperative attitudes began to fade. For example, Dan Lacy, a consistent champion of closer cooperation between publishers and librarians, left the American Book Publishers Council in 1966. Industry leaders after Lacy did not feel as strongly about the importance of publisher-librarian cooperation. Economic pressures in the late 1960s and early 1970s also had an effect. Publishers raised prices to meet increased costs, and as the rate of inflation increased, librarians looked to resource sharing, networking, and more selective book-buying to stretch their limited acquisitions budgets.

Copyright, however, was the single most important issue in the deterioration of publisher-librarian relations, and it rapidly became the divisive issue. A bill for a proposed revision of the copyright law, introduced in 1965, grew more controversial as a decade of hearings progressed, with a few publishers actually going so far as to conclude that "the photocopy machine in the hands of a librarian is the most serious threat to the survival of the publishing industry."[14] The new Copyright Law of 1976 did not stop disputes about "fair use" or decrease uncertainty about the effects of new technological changes.

According to economist Robert W. Frase, "Wall Street discovered book publishing" in the mid-1960s, mainly because of "well-publicized increases in federal support for education and libraries" during the administration of President Lyndon B. Johnson.[15] Conglomerates such as CBS, MCA, Gulf &

Western, the Times-Mirror Corporation, and Xerox gradually entered the industry. The book-publishing business expanded in the 1970s, but the absorption, or in some cases the attempted absorption, of smaller firms by large conglomerates brought forth charges of "undue concentration" from the Authors Guild. It felt that such mergers threatened the "very existence" of the book community. The dispute was aired at congressional hearings held on March 13, 1980, where Senator Howard M. Metzenbaum went a step further and expressed his concern about "greater and greater concentration" in the book*selling* business as well.[16]

The growth of publishing and communication conglomerates heightened distrust. The increased size of many publishing firms, for example, was seen by sociologist Lewis Coser as one reason why so many publishers and major editors seemed to be "losing contact with the world of creative intellect." Coser felt that to the extent that publishers and editors were separated from authors by agents and others, they were likely "to let their general cultural responsibilities remain on the back burner, while the front burner is occupied by business considerations and calculations."[17]

If in the 1970s publishing as a profession turned inward toward business considerations, the library profession continued its inward drive toward further specialization and thus fragmentation. The technological revolution, symbolized by the establishment in 1971 of the first computer-based, online cataloging system, captured the attention of librarians and became a dominant force in the profession. Neither publishers nor librarians seemed able to reach very far beyond their own immediate problems or concerns. Since by then government was in a period of retrenchment, at least in terms of support for education and cultural activities, the decade was an inauspicious time for undertaking cooperative endeavors that would enhance the role of the book in the general culture. Several publishers recognized the need, however. Writing in the April 1977 issue of *Scholarly Publishing,* Herbert S. Bailey, director of the Princeton University Press, explained that while the book community

> should be working together for the advancement of scholarship and for the good of society, we seem to be separated by a system that puts authors and publishers and booksellers and librarians and finally readers in opposition to each other, so that we often offend each other in seeking our individual interests—in copyright, in selecting publications, in making academic appointments, in purchasing, in the prices we charge, (and) in the uses we make of books.[18]

Action came from an unexpected direction in the fall of 1977. At the urging of Librarian of Congress Daniel J. Boorstin, Congress created the Center for the Book in the Library of Congress. Boorstin, a historian who became Librarian of Congress in 1975, was eager for the institution to play a more prominent role in the national culture. In an article in *Harper's* written before he became Librarian of Congress, he had explained in detail why "the book" was the best "do-it-yourself, energy-free communication device" ever invented.[19] The development of a new office at the Library of Congress for promoting books was, for him, a natural and logical action. Representative Lucien N. Nedzi of Michigan and Senator Howard Cannon of Nevada, the chairman and cochairman of the Joint Committee on the Library, cosponsored the necessary legislation. The center was established by Public Law 95-129, approved on October 13, 1977, in which the U.S. Congress affirmed its belief in "the importance of the printed word and the book" and recognized the need for continued study of the book and the written record as "central to our understanding of ourselves and our world." President Jimmy Carter approved the legislation to indicate his "commitment to scholarly research and the development of public interest in books and reading."[20]

The new law authorized the Center for the Book to use private, tax-deductible contributions to support its program and publications. Thus the new organization was founded as a true partnership between government and the private sector. Its initial planning meetings and programs were supported by two generous private donors: McGraw-Hill, Inc., and Mrs. Charles W. Engelhard. Over a dozen people who had been closely associated with the National Book Committee, the Government Advisory Committee on International Book and Library Programs, and Franklin Book Programs became valuable members of the Center for the Book's first National Advisory Board, and their previous experiences helped shape the center's early programs.

There are important differences, however, between the Center for the Book and its organizational predecessors, and perhaps these differences will help ensure a long life for the center. The creation of the Center for the Book was supported by the U.S. Congress and endorsed by the president. The center has the authority of a government agency and enjoys the prestige of being part of the Library of Congress, a unique and most appropriate home for such an endeavor. But it does not depend on government funding for its program; in fact two-thirds of its total annual budget *must* come from private contributions from individuals and corporations. Thus the center has a practical, project-oriented character that is tailored to specific activities which outside donors are willing to support. Finally, the center serves as a catalyst—a source of ideas, a stimulator, and a forum—and does not itself administer any major programs or long-term projects. Its full-time staff consists of only two people. Thus, while it is part of a large and prestigious government institution that also happens to be the world's largest library, the Center for the Book itself is small and flexible—two desirable traits in the fragile and always changing community of the book.

Between 1977 and the present day, the Center for the Book in the Library of Congress has sponsored over two dozen symposia and lectures, two major exhibitions, and over forty publications. Its principal concerns since its founding day have been book and reading development, the history of books, and the contemporary role of books and reading, nationally and internationally. Symposia about important issues in the book world include Television, the Book, and the Classroom (1978), Literacy in Historical Perspective (1980), The Textbook in American Society (1979), The Co-

Responsibilities of American Publishers and Booksellers (1980), and Reading and Successful Living: The Family-School Partnership (1981).

The April 1983 report, *A Nation at Risk,* prepared by the National Commission on Excellence in Education, revived national interest in education and the importance of "a learning society." *A Nation at Risk* stimulated many commissions and reports that addressed different aspects of education, literacy, and the world of books. The Center for the Book's contribution to this national "agenda" of reports, *Books in Our Future* (1984), drew on the thoughts and opinions of many parts of the book community. The conclusions, however, were those of Librarian of Congress Boorstin, who, summarizing his views in the letter of transmittal to the U.S. Congress, pointed out that the Culture of the Book is now threatened, not by technology, but by the "twin menaces" of illiteracy (not being able to read) and aliteracy (not reading even when one knows how). What we do about books and reading in the next decades, he noted, "will crucially affect our citizens' ability to share in the wisdom and delights of civilization, and their capacity for intelligent self-government."[21] *Books in Our Future* is a practical description of "what our citizens are doing and can do" about books and reading, as well as steps that might be taken by the government. Thirty-one organizations are mentioned, and their efforts are cited as "encouraging examples of what we all can do" in order "to keep the Culture of the Book thriving in our country."[22]

This publication briefly describes those thirty-one organizations and the activities of fifty-eight others. Taken together, the efforts of these eighty-nine organizations are the core of the American "community of the book," at least as seen from the Center for the Book in the Library of Congress late in 1985. May our number expand!

Notes

1. John Y. Cole, *The Center for the Book in the Library of Congress: The Planning Year.* (Washington, 1978), 5-6.

2. Daniel J. Boorstin, *A Nation of Readers* (Washington, 1982).

3. Joint Committee on the Library, Congress of the United States, *Books in Our Future: A Report from the Librarian of Congress to the Congress* (Washington, 1984), letter of transmittal.

4. John Y. Cole, *The Center for the Book in the Library of Congress: The Planning Year,* 5-6.

5. Samuel S. Vaughan, "The Community of the Book," *Daedalus,* Winter 1983, 112: 112. For another perspective on "the shared responsibilities of the book community," see Ann Heidbreder Eastman, "Books, Publishing, Libraries in the Information Age," *Library Trends,* Fall 1984, 33:121-47.

6. In learning about events in the United States book community from the 1950s to the present, the author has profited from discussions with many of the key participants, including Dan Lacy, Theodore Waller, Robert W. Frase,

Virginia Mathews, Ann Heidbreder Eastman, and Carol A. Nemeyer. These discussions made the superficial nature of this essay evident and the need for a more detailed oral history of the book community obvious. The Center for the Book is organizing such a project. The first stage will focus on the origins of publishing and library legislation, including international treaties, from World War II to the present.

7. Theodore Waller, "The United States Experience in Promoting Books, Reading, and the International Flow of Information," in John Y. Cole, ed., *The International Flow of Information: A Trans-Pacific Perspective* (Washington, 1981), 14.

8. Waller, "The United States Experience," 15-16.

9. Curtis G. Benjamin, *U.S. Books Abroad: Neglected Ambassadors* (Washington, 1984), 17, 24-25, 34-38.

10. Benjamin, *U.S. Books Abroad*, 20-21.

11. John C. Frantz, "A Death in the Family," *American Libraries*, April 1975, 6: 206.

12. Editorial, "We Shall Miss the National Book Committee," *Publishers Weekly*, December 2, 1974, 15.

13. Benjamin, *U.S. Books Abroad*, 26.

14. Jay K. Lucker, "Publishers and Librarians: Reflections of a Research Library Administrator," *Library Quarterly*, January 1984, 54: 50.

15. Robert W. Frase, tape cassette to John Y. Cole, October 2, 1985.

16. John Y. Cole, ed., *Responsibilities of the American Book Community* (Washington, 1981), 24.

17. Lewis A. Coser, "The Private and Public Responsibilities of the American Publisher," in Cole, ed., *Responsibilities of the American Book Community*, 15.

18. Herbert S. Bailey, Jr., "Economics of Publishing in the Humanities," *Scholarly Publishing*, April 1977, 8: 223-24.

19. Daniel J. Boorstin, "A Design for an Anytime, Do-It-Yourself, Energy Free Communication Device," *Harper's*, January 1974, 83-86.

20. 91 Stat. 1151; Library of Congress *Information Bulletin* 36 (October 21, 1977), 717. Boorstin's initiative was reinforced by a 1976 report of a publishers advisory group, chaired by Dan Lacy of McGraw-Hill, which called on the Library of Congress to strengthen its activities "in relation to the role of the book in American culture." See John Y. Cole, ed., *The Library of Congress in Perspective* (New York: Bowker, 1978), 240-42.

21. *Books in Our Future*, letter of transmittal.

22. *Books in Our Future*, 27-41.

How to Use
This Directory

Carren O. Kaston

The Community of the Book is a descriptive directory of organizations whose activities significantly overlap with the interests of the Center for the Book in the Library of Congress. Alphabetically arranged, the entries provide addresses, telephone numbers, and contact persons for the organizations; general descriptions of their purposes; examples of activities; the names of publications of the organizations; and a description of how the organizations are funded. "A Few Other Resources," located after the alphabetical list, names several publications not found in the main directory and a few organizations too highly specialized to warrant full entries. The index covers the introduction, the directory, and "A Few Other Organizations," including names of organizations, sub-organizations, projects, and individuals as well as giving subject access to the information in this volume.

The directory gives an indication of the enormous diversity of the book community in the United States. Taking as a point of departure the thirty-one organizations listed in the 1984 Library of Congress publication *Books in Our Future*, the directory, though not exhaustive, is intended to serve as a guide to most of the major organizations and programs whose purposes and interests overlap with those of the Center for the Book. Publishers, booksellers, librarians, book researchers, scholars, teachers, and writers are among those represented here by a selective listing of their professional associations. Shared areas of interest include reading skills (the problem of illiteracy) and reading motivation (the problem of aliteracy); the state of the book industry; books and technology; the potential complementarity of books and the media; censorship; the history of books; and the international role of the book.

While some of the groups listed in the directory have, in the past, cosponsored activities with the Center for the Book and others have not, all qualify for inclusion by virtue of their efforts to foster an appreciation of the importance of reading and of books, both historically and in contemporary society. These organizations and programs not only direct their energies to special book constituencies, but also, like the Center for the Book, seek to promote an awareness of books and book-related concerns among a more general audience—the American public. In nurturing a closer relationship between those who create books and those who read them, these organizations thus have in common their effort to reach out and make the community of the book even larger.

Directory entries feature the outreach activities and strategies of these various organizations and programs. At the head of each entry is a block of basic data that includes the name and address of the organization; the telephone number, name, and title of the person to contact for additional information; and the year in which the organization was founded. Beneath this block are four narrative sections: *What/For Whom, Examples, Publications,* and *Sources of Support.* The *What/For Whom* section presents an overview of the organization, describing what it is, whom it serves, and what it does for them. Descriptions are based largely on materials that were provided by the organizations and programs themselves. *Examples* is in most cases the heart of the entry in terms of the community of the book. It focuses on those projects that illustrate the organization's reading and book promotion activities, particularly among general audiences. The *Examples* section thus fleshes out those aims and interests that, as a member of the book community, the organization or program shares with the Center for the Book. The *Publications* section focuses on printed materials related to reading and books. *Sources of Support* may stimulate in readers ideas for projects they can adapt to their own organizational needs and structures.

Organizations
and Programs

Cross-references to other organizations are given in the directory by entry number (§).

§1   ACTION

806 Connecticut Avenue, N.W.
Washington, D.C. 20525
202-634-9135
Established in 1971

What/For Whom ACTION is the principal agency in the federal government for administering volunteer service programs. It operates through ten regional offices. Its programs are authorized by the Domestic Volunteer Service Act of 1973 as amended, and several of them have a literacy component.

Examples 1) Older American Volunteer Program. The department runs three programs that include literacy training: the Foster Grandparent Program, the Senior Companion Program, and the Retired Senior Volunteer Program. Of these, the Retired Senior Volunteer Program (RSVP) has the largest literacy project. RSVP provides opportunities for retired men and women, aged sixty and over, to serve on a regular basis in a variety of settings throughout their communities. Senior volunteers are part-time and do not receive stipends. They work under the auspices of an established community service organization with funding, support and technical assistance provided by ACTION and the local community. For further information, contact Janet Farbstein, Literacy Specialist, 202-634-9353.

2) Volunteers in Service to America (VISTA). Diana London, Chief, 202-634-9424. VISTA added literacy training to its program when Congress passed a series of amendments to the legislation in May 1984. Between one-fifth and one-fourth of VISTA's programs and participating volunteers are involved in literacy assistance for lower-income adults, both English-speaking and non–English-speaking. They recruit and train tutors, help to generate private-sector resources, identify those needing literacy assistance, and promote community awareness and support. Although some are independent, many of VISTA's literacy efforts are coordinated with those of Laubach Literacy Action (§ 52) and Literacy Volunteers of America (§ 54) around the country. The average volunteer age is presently in the late thirties, but anyone eighteen or older is eligible. Volunteers work full-time for a full year and are paid a subsistence stipend.

3) Young Volunteers in Action (YVA). Barbara Wyatt, Director, 202-634-9410. Students between the ages of fourteen and twenty-two volunteer to help low-income people in their local communities in different areas of need, providing services to young children, senior citizens, the disabled, latchkey children, refugees, and illiterates, among others. Roughly two-thirds of the currently funded projects have a literacy component. Student volunteers serve on a part-time basis and without a stipend, but receive some financial support from their local

19

communities. Unlike RSVP programs, which can be funded continuously, YVA projects are funded by the federal government for no more than two years.

4) Office of Policy and Planning. Jeffrey Hammer, Director of Policy Development, 202-634-9287. Through this office, ACTION funds demonstration grants related to voluntarism. Recent grants here supported projects concerned with drug abuse, runaway youth, neighborhood initiatives, and illiteracy. The focus is on innovative—and sometimes experimental— ways of dealing with social problems, and the demonstration projects that are funded must have the potential for widespread use. A recent literacy grant, for example, funded the development of films to teach literacy trainers in rural areas.

Source of Support   Federal government.

---

§2   Action for Children's Television (ACT)

46 Austin Street
Newtonville, Massachusetts 02160
617-527-7870
Peggy Charren, *Director*
Established in 1968

What/For Whom   Action for Children's Television is a national nonprofit child advocacy group that works to encourage diversity in children's television programming and to eliminate abuses in advertising aimed at children. ACT initiates legal reform and promotes public awareness of issues relating to children's television through public education campaigns, publications, national conferences, and speaking engagements. ACT's efforts to improve broadcasting practices related to children include filing petitions with the Federal Communications Commission and the Federal Trade Commission, testifying before the Congress in favor of legislation (e.g., the Children's Television Education Act), working with the television industry itself, and cooperating with professional associations concerned with children's welfare. ACT Awards highlight achievements in children's television. ACT resources books provide information on special subjects in children's programming, including the arts, consumerism, stereotyping, children who are disabled, role models, and the sciences. The ACT Resource Library is open to the public by appointment and contains publications on children's television representing the views of broadcasters, advertisers, major scientific researchers, child specialists, and consumer groups.

Examples   1) In 1980, ACT and the Center for the Book in the Library of Congress cosponsored the symposium "Broadcasting Books to

Young Audiences," in which authors, editors, producers, broadcasters, and librarians explored ways of developing more children's television programming based on books. As an outgrowth of the conference, ACT asked publishers of children's books to choose books they have published that would make good television programs. The suggestions were published by ACT as *Editors' Choice: A Look at Books for Children's TV* (1982).

2) As an extension of that project, ACT in 1984 solicited lists of children's books that could be used for national programming about the bicentennial of the U.S. Consitution and the Bill of Rights in 1987.

Publications Many bibliographies, resource books, and handbooks.

Sources of Support Membership contributions; gifts from foundations, corporations, and public agencies.

---

§3 Adult Performance Level Project (APL)

College of Education—Education Annex Suite 21
University of Texas at Austin
Austin, Texas 78712
512-471-4623
Jim C. Cates, *Director*
Established in 1971

What/For Whom "Adult Performance Level" is an educational concept that emerged from research begun in 1971 at the University of Texas with funding from the U.S. Department of Health, Education, and Welfare. The objectives of the research project were to describe adult functional literacy in pragmatic, behavioral terms and to develop instruments for measuring functional competency. Other products of the research included a skills curriculum to teach functional competency and a competency-based high school diploma program that awards a regular diploma for the demonstration of these skills. APL offers technical assistance and training to literacy organizations in the establishment, administration, and evaluation of this Competency-Based Curriculum and High School Diploma (CBHSD) Program.

Publications *Final Report: The Adult Performance Level Study,* published in 1977, presents the findings of the study funded by the Department of Health, Education, and Welfare. APL's instructional system is published by Harcourt Brace Jovanovich under the title *The APL Series: Coping in Today's Society.*

Sources of Support Publications, training and consulting fees, royalties, and administrative support from the University of Texas.

21

§4 American Antiquarian Society (AAS)

185 Salisbury Street
Worcester, Massachusetts 01609-1634
617-755-5221
Marcus A. McCorison, *Director and Librarian*
Established in 1812

What/For Whom

The American Antiquarian Society is an important research library that specializes in American history to 1877. The AAS holds approximately two-thirds of the items known to have been printed in this country between 1640 and 1821, as well as the most useful source materials and reference works printed since that period. The collections serve a worldwide community of students, teachers, historians, bibliographers, genealogists, and authors whose work at the society reaches a broad audience through textbooks, biographies, historical novels, newspapers, periodicals, plays, films, and library programs. In addition, the society's own library staff produces scholarship, for example, a history of printing in America, a history and bibliography of American newspapers, and the standard work on Paul Revere's engravings, as well as family genealogies and first editions of American literature.

Example

The Program in the History of the Book in American Culture, established in 1983, is aimed at stimulating research and education in this interdisciplinary field. The program sponsors scholarly activities, including annual lectures, workshops, conferences, publications, and residential fellowships. The society's first annual Summer Seminar in the History of the Book in American Culture, entitled "The Making of Literate America: Diffusion of Culture Based on Printing, 1750–1850," focused on the activities in the book trade of AAS founder Isaiah Thomas. A 1984 colloquium focused on literacy and numeracy among children in seventeenth-century New England.

Publications

The AAS *News-Letter*, monthly; and *The Book*, the newsletter of the Program in the History of the Book in America Culture, three times a year. *Printing and Society in Early America* (1983), the proceedings of a 1980 conference, was the first publication sponsored by the Program in the History of the Book in American Culture.

Sources of Support

Private support and federal grants.

§5 American Association for Adult and Continuing Education (AAACE)

1201 16th Street, N.W., Suite 230
Washington, D.C. 20036
202-822-7866
Judith A. Koloski, *Executive Director*
Established in 1982

What/For Whom

AAACE is a private, nonprofit national service organization for professionals in the fields of adult and continuing education. Services include conferences, advocacy, dissemination of information, research, and staff development and training. The association offers programs in literacy, adult basic education, and English as a Second Language, as well as in adult and continuing education. Staff development and training services focus especially on training teachers how to teach adults to read and think critically. The association's Division of State, Local and Institutional Management contains the National Council of State Directors of Adult Education (NCSDAE), which, through a network of government-funded literacy programs in every state, provides professional classroom instruction to over two million adults in need of basic reading skills. The Division of State, Local and Institutional Management also includes the Administrators of Adult Education, which provides similar services at the local level.

Examples

1) Coalition for Literacy (§36). AAACE and NCSDAE are among the eleven national literacy and education organizations in the Coalition for Literacy.

2) Life Skills Program. The program includes the Commission on Adult Basic Education, which focuses on literacy and English as a Second Language.

3) AAACE received a grant from the Business Council for Effective Literacy (§26) to anticipate the impact of the Coalition for Literacy's National Awareness Campaign on the resource and funding needs of literacy programs nationwide. AAACE's findings are now available in the Business Council publication *Turning Illiteracy Around: An Agenda for National Action.*

Publications

The *AAACE Newsletter;* two journals, *Lifelong Learning* and *Adult Education Quarterly;* a variety of pamphlets and books on current issues in adult and continuing education, including *Toward New Partnerships in Basic Education for the Workplace* (forthcoming), based on a series of workshops for business and education leaders.

Sources of Support

Membership dues, conferences, publications, foundation grants.

§6 American Association of Retired Persons (AARP)

1909 K Street, N.W.
Washington, D.C. 20049
202-872-4700
Established in 1958

What/For Whom

AARP is the oldest and largest service and advocacy organization of older Americans, representing roughly one-fourth of all Americans over the age fifty-five. Its purpose is to improve the quality of life for older Americans through efforts in such areas as age discrimination, health care, consumer affairs, crime prevention, tax assistance, research on aging, and adult continuing education. AARP legislative specialists lobby for the interests of older Americans at both state and federal levels. Membership is open to anyone aged fifty or older, whether retired or not.

Examples

1) Book Purchase Project. To commemorate the twenty-fifth anniversary of the national organization, AARP established a nationwide Book Purchase Project in 1983. Aimed at young children and teenagers, the program enables local AARP chapters to donate to secondary school and community libraries books that will help dispel unwarranted stereotypes about aging. Novels, biographies, essays, and plays, recommended by the national headquarters, help students recognize the capabilities of older people and become more aware of their own aging and development. A second benefit of the program is that members of the local AARP chapter become better acquainted with their community's library resources. The Reference and Adult Services Division, a division of the American Library Association (§13), is participating in AARP's Book Purchase Project through informational news releases to the library press and by helping to distribute to local AARP chapters the lists of books recommended for use in the project. For further information about the Book Purchase Project, contact Leo Baldwin, Senior Coordinator of Special Projects in the Program Department of AARP, 202-728-4375.

2) Institute of Lifetime Learning. The institute is AARP's continuing education service. It promotes learning opportunities for older people, helps prepare them for new careers, and promotes their involvement in media and new technologies. The institute's Center on Education and Aging offers counsel and resource services to AARP chapters, educational institutions, libraries, industry, and individuals interested in initiating programs for older persons. In addition, the institute collects information on literacy organizations and issues as they affect all age groups. Currently the institute is exploring the use of technology in instruction for older people. For further information, contact Dennis LaBuda, Director, Institute of Lifetime

Learning, 1133 20th Street, N.W., Washington, D.C. 20005,
202-662-4895

Publications Two bimonthly magazines, *Modern Maturity* and *Dynamic Years*,
as well as the monthly *AARP News Bulletin*.

Sources of Support Membership dues, magazine subscriptions, investments, sale of
advertising.

§7 American Black Book Writers Association, Inc. (ABBWA)

P.O. Box 10548
Marina del Rey, California 90295
213-822-5195
Will Gibson, *President*
Established in 1979

What/For Whom The American Black Book Writers Association is a national,
nonprofit organization dedicated to furthering the works and
careers of black book writers and advancing and preserving
black literature in general. "Black book writers" are defined as
black writers and other writers whose books have a particular
relevance or appeal to the black community. ABBWA's goals
are to increase awareness of books in the black community
and, ultimately, to bring about a black literary renaissance.
Most immediately, the association's focus is on strengthening
the black book market, on the assumption that if the publishing of black books is more profitable, more books by and for
blacks will be published. ABBWA members are publishers;
writers, regardless of race; and other interested individuals.

In order to increase the number of black books being published and read, ABBWA plans to issue a regularly updated
catalog of black book titles; publish a Black Book Review; conduct black book exhibitions and bookfairs; assist prison literary
programs; work closely with anti-illiteracy programs; and
develop ABBWA racks for bookstores, with cooperative advertising. The association maintains close working relationships
with African and Caribbean writers; provides assistance, especially to young or unpublished writers; offers members a
manuscript evaluation service; and is beginning to conduct
community education efforts, particularly among black youth.

Examples 1) Black Book Council. ABBWA is in the process of establishing the Black Book Council, which will promote an annual
Black Book Month; give national Black Book Awards, especially for children's books; support large-type books for black

seniors; create a directorate of African and Caribbean affairs for black writer and market development; give loans and grants for the publishing of black manuscripts; encourage the publishing of local histories; and conduct research and studies of black books. Consciously modeled after the Jewish Book Council's efforts on behalf of Jewish books, the Black Book Council is intended to foster an environment in which good black books can flourish.

2) Anticensorship program. The association opposes book banning as a solution to the problem of alleged racism in books.

3) Special reports on black book publishing. The first report, "Nigeria: A Book Export Surprise," deals with American book sales in Africa. A study is currently being conducted on the role good books can play in the war against illiteracy in the black ghetto.

4) ABBWA's Lecture Bureau links speakers with organizations to arrange lectures on topics of interest.

Publications

ABBWA Journal, quarterly, is a journal for the black book industry that emphasizes publishing and marketing concerns. It includes a book review section.

Sources of Support

Membership dues, corporate and foundation grants, and contributions.

§8 American Booksellers Association (ABA)

122 East 42d Street
New York, New York 10168
212-867-9060
Bernard Rath, *Executive Director*
Established in 1900

What/For Whom

The American Booksellers Association's purpose is "to define and strengthen the position of the book retailer in the book distribution chain." Its members are individuals and firms engaged in the retail sale of books in the United States. Association activities include promoting the retail sale of books, fostering sound bookseller-publisher relations, aiding booksellers in the encouragement of reading at all age levels, and representing the interests of booksellers on legal issues, such as First Amendment concerns and alleged unfair trade practices. The ABA also sponsors national conferences, as well as educational seminars and workshops on bookselling for its membership.

Examples

1) In the past two years, the ABA has shown increasing interest in the problem of illiteracy. "Toward a Reading Society" was the theme of its 1985 annual convention and trade exhibit. "Give the Gift of Literacy" is the theme of the 1986 convention and a major, ABA-sponsored national effort to raise public consciousness about the problem of illiteracy in the United States. Money collected in the 1986 "Give the Gift of Literacy" campaign will be equally divided between Reading is Fundamental (§75) and the Coalition for Literacy (§36).

2) "Book-Shop! '85." In 1985, for the second year, ABA placed a Christmas advertising insert in *Time* magazine to emphasize the virtues of books as gifts.

3) The Media Coalition. The coalition, consisting of trade associations of publishers, distributors, and retailers in the print media, by lobbying and litigation combats attempts to censor the sale of certain books and periodicals.

4) Banned Books Week. Banned Books Week is cosponsored annually by the ABA, the American Library Association (§13), the National Association of College Stores (§59), the Association of American Publishers (§20), and the American Society of Journalists and Authors. Its goal is to highlight books that have been banned, thus attracting media attention to threats against the First Amendment and the importance of the freedom to read.

5) ABA's 1985 booksellers merchandising effort, which provides display and merchandising materials to participating member bookstores, borrowed some themes from the Center for the Book in the Library of Congress (§30). A literacy promotion effort featured a poster facsimile of the Library's recently-issued "Nation of Readers" postage stamp, which shows President Abraham Lincoln reading to his son, Tad; bookstore events nationwide tied in with a CBS-TV "Read More About It" program on space exploration. The "Nation of Readers" poster also served as the focus of the Bookstore Merchandising Group's contest for the most creative and visually effective window or in-store display.

Publications

ABA Newswire is a comprehensive weekly newsletter for booksellers that lists forthcoming publicity about books and authors. It contains succinct information about TV and radio appearances, lectures, articles, and book reviews, as well as major advertising and promotional offers. *American Bookseller,* a monthly magazine of news and features of interest to booksellers, includes a section on "Books & the Media," providing summaries of current and upcoming movies and television programs that have a connection to books. *Basic Book List,* a periodically revised list of staple hardbound and paperback titles recommended as a nucleus for a bookstore's basic stock, reflects actual sales records in bookstores across the country.

Sources of Support

Membership dues and trade exhibits.

§9   American Council of Learned Societies (ACLS)

228 East 45th Street, 16th Floor
New York, New York 10017
212-697-1505
R. M. Lumiansky, *President Pro Tempore*
Established in 1919

What/For Whom

The American Council of Learned Societies is a federation of national organizations concerned with the humanities and the humanistic elements of the social sciences. Its forty-five members are scholarly associations in areas of language, literature, philosophy, religion, history, the arts, law, political science, sociology, and psychology. ACLS promotes the humanities through fellowships, grants-in-aid, and travel and exchange awards to scholars; investigations into the needs of humanistic scholarship; and cooperation both nationally and internationally with other organizations. The ACLS Office of Scholarly Communication and Technology (§10) was opened in 1984 to study and promote the system of scholarly communication.

Examples

1) With the Social Science Research Council, ACLS sponsors the International Research and Exchanges Board, which is responsible for several scholarly exchange programs with Eastern European countries. The aim is to enable U.S. scholars to study in Eastern Europe and the USSR and to enable Eastern scholars to study in the United States.

2) The ACLS has directed the preparation of several large-scale, vital reference works, the *Dictionary of American Biography,* the *Dictionary of Scientific Biography,* and the *Dictionary of the Middle Ages,* which is now being published.

Publications

A quarterly newsletter and an annual report.

Sources of Support

Grants from foundations, the National Endowment for the Humanities, and corporations; fees from members and a number of colleges and universities that are associate members.

§10 American Council of Learned Societies — Office of Scholarly Communication and Technology

1717 Massachusetts Avenue, N.W., Suite 401
Washington, D.C. 20036
202-328-2431
Herbert C. Morton, *Director*
Founded in 1984

What/For Whom

The Office of Scholarly Communication and Technology of the American Council of Learned Societies encourages the participation of scholars in activities related to scholarly communication. ACLS (§9) is a federation of national associations concerned with the humanities. The Office of Scholarly Communication aims at promoting cooperation among scholars, publishers, librarians, and university administrators; monitoring changes in the system of scholarly communication; studying this system and its effectiveness; and studying the effects of technological change on the thinking and working of scholars.

Examples

1) Preparation of an annotated bibliography of about 100 items on scholarly communication is underway. The bibliography will focus on (1) scholarly publishing, including both books and journals, and its changing markets and technologies; (2) libraries, particularly the impact of online cataloging and the problems of preservation; and (3) other areas, like copyright and photocopying, where there seem to be conflicts among various participants.

2) The office sponsors surveys, studies, and conferences and workshops on problems in scholarly communication.

Publications

A newsletter, *Scholarly Communication;* a series of reprints on scholarly communication, now underway; other reports are planned.

Sources of Support

ACLS; private foundations; National Endowment for the Humanities.

§11 American Federation of Labor-Congress of Industrial Organizations (AFL-CIO)

815 16th Street, N.W.
Washington, D.C. 20006
202-637-5144
Jim Auerbach, *AFL-CIO Department of Education*
Established in 1955

What/For Whom

The American Federation of Labor–Congress of Industrial Organizations (AFL–CIO) represents American labor in world affairs through participation in international labor bodies. It coordinates such activities as community services, political education, and voter education. Sometimes referred to as a "union of unions," the AFL–CIO is a voluntary federation of roughly one hundred national and international unions representing thousands of local unions.

The AFL–CIO has a long tradition of cooperation with libraries in its programming and publications, especially in providing library service to labor groups. It has also actively promoted literacy and basic skill training through its own Department of Education. The federation's concern with literacy has been intensified by a long period of structural unemployment nationwide, in which those displaced and laid-off workers who are also illiterate have suffered the additional handicap of being unable to qualify for retraining programs. The AFL–CIO therefore emphasizes retraining that is linked to adult literacy and basic education programs.

Examples

1) AFL–CIO/American Library Association (ALA) Joint Committee on Library Service to Labor Groups. The joint committee with the American Library Association (§13) was established to foster closer cooperation between librarians and labor organizations. It promotes awareness of common interests among librarians and labor educators and encourages wider and more intensive patronage of libraries by members of the labor community and their families. In recent years, the joint committee has published a bibliography for librarians and others to use in building a library collection about labor, as well as bibliographies on workplace health and safety and on women workers. The committee also gives programs and sponsors film and materials exhibits at ALA conferences. One recent program, for example, focused on ways in which libraries can serve the unemployed during recession and recovery. The joint committee actively supports the ALA's National Library Week.

30

2) In 1981, the ALA established the John Sessions Memorial Award for a library with outstanding programs for labor unions in its community. John Sessions was Assistant Director of the AFL–CIO Department of Education and was very active on the joint committee.

3) Many local union programs address the problem of literacy. For example, since 1971, District Council 37 has used an education fund it negotiated with the City of New York to offer programs in high school equivalency diploma training, career training, and adult literacy. Classes are given at union headquarters and in training centers established at public schools, hospitals, and other institutions.

4) The Service Employees International Union has a Lifelong Education and Development (LEAD) Program, developed in 1978 under a grant from the U.S. Department of Labor, which addresses needs in high school equivalency training, career advancement, and adult literacy, including English as a second language. In many cases, LEAD proposals have been included in contracts as employer contributions. For additional information, contact Deborah Ness, Director, Lifelong Education and Development (LEAD), Service Employees International Union AFL–CIO, 2020 K Street, N.W., Washington, D.C. 20006, 202-452-8750.

Publications   *Education Update,* monthly reports prepared by the AFL–CIO Department of Education on labor conferences, workshops, new publications, and other resources; various pamphlets and bibliographies.

Source of Support   Union dues.

---

§12   American Institute of Graphic Arts (AIGA)

1059 Third Avenue
New York, New York 10021
212-752-0813
Caroline Hightower, *Director*
Established in 1914

What/For Whom   The American Institute of Graphic Arts is a national nonprofit organization of graphic design and graphic arts professionals. It conducts an interrelated program of competitions, exhibitions, publications, educational activities, and projects in the public interest in order to promote excellence in, and the advancement of, the graphic design profession. Institute

31

members are involved in the design and production of books, magazines, and periodicals as well as corporate, environmental, and promotional graphics. Their contribution of specialized skills and expertise provides the foundation for the institute's programs. AIGA's first national conference was in 1985, though competitions, exhibitions, publications, and educational activities have been held for some time.

Examples

1) The Book Show is one of two annual AIGA shows (a number of others are held less often). Competition for the show makes acceptance one of the most prestigious awards for book design. Books accepted for the show appear in *AIGA Graphic Design USA*.

2) AIGA annually contributes exhibitions to the Low Library at Columbia University, helping to provide an ongoing archive of graphic design in America.

Publications

Journal of Graphic Design, which regularly publishes articles on the graphic arts and graphic design; *AIGA Graphic Design USA,* an annual recording the work selected in the year's national competitions for exhibition; and other professional publications.

Sources of Support

Membership dues, corporate sponsors, subscriptions, sale of publications, and federal grants (for the national conference).

§13 American Library Association (ALA)

50 East Huron Street
Chicago, Illinois 60611
312-944-6780
Peggy Barber, *Associate Executive Director for Communications*
Established in 1876

What/For Whom

The American Library Association is the oldest and largest library association in the world. In addition to librarians, its 40,000 members include library educators and researchers, publishers, and the general public. Its members represent all types of libraries: public, school, academic, and special—the libraries that serve governments, businesses, and armed services, hospitals, prisons, and other institutions. ALA's goals include improving library services, promoting reading, promoting the public awareness of libraries, increasing the accessibility of information, protecting the right to read, and monitoring and improving the education of librarians.

32

1) National Library Week. ALA's biggest annual promotion effort is National Library Week, held in April. Each year, ALA's Public Information Office selects a theme, prepares promotional television and radio spots, posters, and other materials, and creates a kit for distribution to librarians throughout the United States. Some effort goes toward national publicity, but the greatest emphasis is on enabling local libraries of all kinds to enlist local support in promoting libraries and library use. National Library Week Partners is an organization of about sixty-five associations, organizations, and businesses that support National Library Week. The 1985 theme for National Library Week was "A Nation of Readers," programs for which included a photo contest and exhibit at the Library of Congress. The 1986 theme is "Get a Head Start at the Library."

2) "Let's Talk About It: Reading and Discussion Programs in America's Libraries" is a series of book discussion programs held in local libraries throughout the United States. A program of the Association of Specialized and Cooperative Library Agencies, a division of the ALA, "Let's Talk About It" groups have met at more than three hundred libraries. Adult discussion groups on particular themes, led by local humanities scholars, meet over a ten-week period. This project is funded by the National Endowment for the Humanities (§67), which has also developed manuals and support materials available for local and statewide use after the national project ends in September 1986.

3) Posters promoting libraries, books, and reading are available from ALA.

4) Booklists, many of them pamphlets, are available from ALA. These are selective lists of readings, some arranged by topic, others by audience (adults, young adults, children). Some are not only selective, but the results of awards selections.

5) The Office for Intellectual Freedom coordinates ALA programs in the areas of intellectual freedom and censorship. ALA cosponsors an annual Banned Books Week with the American Booksellers Association (§8), the American Society of Journalists and Authors, the Association of American Publishers (§20), and the National Association of College Stores (§59). ALA also founded the Freedom to Read Foundation (§42), which supplies legal support to librarians and others engaged in First Amendment-related struggles.

6) The Office for Library Outreach Services trains resource personnel who in turn train others in the library field to develop and conduct literacy programs. Management of the Coalition for Literacy (§36) is a major function of this office.

7) ALA/Elderhostel Project. This project arranges for a special edition of the catalog prepared by Elderhostel, Inc. (§40) to be mailed to public libraries across the country three times a year.

8) Awards. The Association for Library Service to Children, a division of ALA, annually awards the Newbery Medal for the year's most distinguished contribution to American literature for children and the Caldecott Medal for the year's most distinguished picture book for children. ALA makes many other awards, most for improvements and progress in librarianship.

9) The Resources and Technical Services Division is deeply involved in efforts to study means of preserving books.

Publications

American Libraries, monthly, is a magazine received by all ALA members that covers the breadth of ALA's interests with news and feature articles. Each of ALA's divisions publishes a journal and many publish newsletters besides. *Booklist* provides prepublication book reviews for public libraries; *Choice* does this for college and university libraries. ALA publishes many books in library management and lists of recommended books. The Office for Intellectual Freedom publishes a bimonthly newsletter, which offers articles and news reports on censorship, primarily in the United States but with some international coverage.

Sources of Support

Membership fees; endowment income; conference proceeds; grants from foundations and government agencies.

---

§14

American Newspaper Publishers Association Foundation (ANPA Foundation)

The Newspaper Center
Box 17407
Dulles International Airport
Washington, D.C. 20041
703-620-9500
Judith D. Hines, *Vice President and Director*
Established in 1961

What/For Whom

The American Newspaper Publishers Association Foundation is a public nonprofit educational foundation devoted to strengthening the press in America. Its programs encompass three principal goals: advancing professionalism in the press through support for journalism education; fostering public understanding of a free press; and cultivating future newspaper readers.

The Newspaper in Education (NIE) program, a major ANPA service, aids parents and educators in teaching young people the fundamentals of reading and of informed citizenship. The NIE program is a cooperative effort between daily newspapers and thousands of U.S. and Canadian schools that use the newspapers to teach a variety of subjects: social studies, math, history, and English, as well as reading. ANPA is a coordinating agency for these local programs. It develops and distributes materials, sponsors conferences for developing NIE programs, and advises individual schools and newspapers. The newspapers themselves provide copies of their papers to schools at discount prices, offer curriculum materials and teacher training, and generally help schools develop newspaper use for student learning.

As a supporter of freedom of the press, the ANPA Foundation is a sponsoring member of the First Amendment Congress, an organization composed of all major professional journalism organizations and committed to enhancing Americans' awareness of the importance of freedom of expression in a democratic society. ANPA acts as the administrative service arm of the congress and publishes its newsletter. It also awards grants to support groups such as the Reporters Committee for Freedom of the Press and the World Press Freedom Committee.

Examples

1) National NIE Week. Annually cosponsored by the International Reading Association (§51) and the ANPA Foundation in cooperation with state and regional press associations, National Newspaper in Education Week promotes the teaching of reading in the classroom through the use of newspapers.

2) Newspaper Readership Project. This two-year study of the NIE program showed that students using newspapers in the classroom registered positive changes in newspaper reading behavior and demonstrated greater interest in and knowledge of current events.

3) Newspaper Literacy Meeting. In March 1985, ANPA's efforts on behalf of literacy resulted in a meeting intended to explore the question "What Can the Newspaper Industry Do to Help Combat Illiteracy?"

Publications

Various NIE publications, including teacher guides and curriculum materials to advance the classroom use of newspapers, among them the booklet "Using Newspapers to Teach Reading Skills"; *Update NIE*, a monthly report; and *Teaching with Newspapers*, a monthly newsletter for methods instructors.

Sources of Support

NIE programs and publications income; sale of promotional material; and proceeds from the foundation's endowment fund, which is supported by contributions from newspapers, newspaper organizations, and individuals in the newspaper business.

§15 American Printing History Association (APHA)

P.O. Box 4922, Grand Central Station
New York, New York 10163
212-673-8770
Philip Sperling, *Treasurer*
Founded in 1974

What/For Whom

The American Printing History Association aims at promoting the study of printing and publishing history. A nonprofit membership organization, APHA has members from throughout the book world, for example book collectors, librarians, printers, editors, private press owners, and historians. APHA sponsors exhibits and conferences, compiles statistics, conducts censuses of artifacts and archives, and presents an annual award for an outstanding contribution to printing history. APHA both coordinates projects in the history of printing and encourages the preservation of the artifacts of the printing trade by museums. Semiannual meetings are held in New York.

Examples

1) The fall conferences of APHA have each focused on a topic in printing history. The 1985 conference had "Printing Without Type" as its theme.

2) In 1976, the Education Committee of APHA surveyed the teaching of the history of books and printing in American graduate schools of library science.

Publications

The APHA Letter is a bimonthly newsletter covering the full range of APHA's interests with news about conferences, lectures, exhibitions, grants, and publications. Queries from members doing research or seeking particular equipment appear, as do offerings of small press equipment for sale. *Printing History* is a semiannual journal with longer articles.

Sources of Support

Membership dues, contributions, sale of publications.

§16   American Reading Council, Ltd.

20 West 40th Street
New York, New York 10018
212-730-0786
Julia Reed Palmer, *Executive Director*
Established in 1976

What/For Whom

The American Reading Council promotes reading and literacy by running demonstration programs at selected community sites, disseminating information about effective literacy programs, and conducting lobbying and advocacy activities in New York State and nationwide. Dissemination of information about literacy was recently expanded to include public service announcements on CBS–TV and WNEW–TV. The council focuses on young children and their parents and teachers, although some literacy work is also done with adults who are illiterate. Methods favored by the council include founding paperback school bookstores, especially in areas where commercial bookstores are nonexistent; forming classroom libraries; planning to place adult volunteers in the classroom; and encouraging periods of Silent Sustained Reading in all schools.

Examples

1) School Library Campaign. This effort encourages the strengthening of existing school libraries and the development of new libraries in the public school system. The assumption behind the project is that many children do not become readers while in school because they see only textbooks or workbooks and are not introduced, through school libraries, to reading for pleasure or information.

2) The Friendly Place/El Sitio Simpatico. The centerpiece of this East Harlem family learning center is a community-based paperback library of thirty thousand titles and a bookstore that carries low-cost books. Preschoolers and their parents are introduced to books through educational play groups, a parenting section in the library, and a sales section of preschool books. There are also satellite libraries in nearby preschool and senior citizen centers.

3) First Reading Program. This public school kindergarten program teaches children aged three to six to read by having them build on their own experiences and also by immersing them in children's literature. Classroom and parent libraries are a part of the program.

4) Adult Literacy Program. This three-year New York City program is designed for young mothers who read below the fifth-grade level. The American Reading Council hopes that the program will also help break the cycle of illiteracy by teaching mothers to help their children become literate.

Sources of Support

Contributions from foundations, corporations, and individuals.

37

§17 Antiquarian Booksellers Association of America (ABAA)

50 Rockefeller Plaza
New York, New York 10020
212-757-9395
Janice M. Farina, *Administrative Assistant*
Founded in 1949

What/For Whom

The Antiquarian Booksellers Association of America is an association for the United States rare book trade. Its members are dealers in rare and out-of-print books. ABAA sponsors regional rare books fairs for the trade in New York, Los Angeles, San Francisco, Chicago, and Boston. ABAA comments on proposed legislation relevant to its members, maintains relations with other organizations concerned with rare books, and sets guidelines for professional conduct for dealers. It also maintains an Antiquarian Booksellers' Benevolent Fund.

Publications

The Professional Rare Bookseller, a journal whose publication is currently suspended, provides articles, news of the trade, and news of the ABAA. ABAA publishes a directory of its members and a pamphlet, *Guidelines for the Antiquarian Booksellers Association of America,* which concerns professional ethics.

Source of Support

Membership fees.

§18 Assault on Illiteracy Program (AOIP)

410 Central Park West (PH-C)
New York, New York 10025
212-867-0898
Emille Smith, *Administrative Coordinator*
Established in 1982

What/For Whom

AOIP is a major effort on the part of the black community to eradicate illiteracy. Not itself an organization, AOIP is a national network for communication and cooperation among more than eighty black-led national organizations, most of them with long-standing literacy programs. They serve mainly black and hispanic youths and adults, especially those whom other programs find it most difficult to reach.

Because they believe that illiteracy among blacks is the product of social and psychological damage caused by racial inequality, participating organizations pursue a two-pronged campaign that includes both literacy tutoring and "community-building." Community-building counters low self-esteem by focusing on the local achievements of black businesses, institutions, and professionals, as reported in black-owned AOIP-participating newspapers. AOIP reading materials correspondingly seek to motivate students through an ego-strengthening "Who Am I?" theme.

AOIP-participating organizations conduct their literacy programs in such community-based sites as neighborhood centers, housing project community rooms, individual homes, workplaces, hospitals, nursing homes, prisons, libraries, public schools, and other public facilities. On the national level, AOIP sponsors public and professional workshops; develops public education materials for use in various media; and develops and evaluates technical material used by students and teachers.

Example

AOIP/USEd Task Force. Although AOIP believes in waging its campaign against illiteracy primarily at the local level, it has established a working relationship with the U.S. Department of Education (§83) to help carry out the Adult Literacy Initiative (§84) announced by President Reagan.

Publications

AOIP communicates with its network through several newspaper operations. The first is a series of AOIP-participating community newspapers primarily associated with Black Media, Inc., a group of publishers responsible for the founding of AOIP. If no local participating paper exists in an area where demand is great, however, AOIP will help to create a local edition of its national newspaper, *Greater News*. At the national level, AOIP's communication needs are also served by the *National Black Monitor*. All of these newspapers emphasize community-building news about black achievements and include an eight-page educational supplement called *The Advancer*.

Sources of Support

The black-owned, community-building newspapers associated with AOIP are the major source of all AOIP funding. Not only do the newspapers print at cost and carry The Advancer each week, but, in addition, their publishers have committed themselves to carrying, free of charge, AOIP and all community-building news from the AOIP-participating organizations in their area. In turn, individual members of local AOIP-participating organizations are committed to subscribe. Additional support for AOIP comes from optional membership contributions by participating organizations.

§19 Association for Community-Based Education (ACBE)

1806 Vernon Street, N.W.
Washington, D.C. 20009
202-462-6333
Christofer P. Zachariadis, *Executive Director*
Established in 1976

What/For Whom

The Association for Community-Based Education is a national membership organization serving and representing community-based educational institutions and programs for nontraditional learners, the disadvantaged, and minorities. ACBE member institutions include accredited colleges, economic development organizations, adult learning programs, literacy projects, and advocacy organizations. Their educational efforts are carried out in the context of community development and community control of local affairs. Typically located in low-income communities, they serve people whose needs are not being met by more established institutions.

Services to member organizations include loans and mini-grants, technical assistance, an annual conference, regional meetings, advocacy, and a clearinghouse to collect and disseminate information about community-based education and its needs for resources. Adult literacy services, most often in a group setting, have traditionally been part of the educational efforts of roughly half of ACBE's member groups.

Example

An ACBE special project in community-based literacy is aimed at linking up the various programs across the country and generating recognition and support for their work. In 1983, supported by B. Dalton Bookseller, ACBE conducted a six-month study of community-based literacy programs, member and nonmember, operating around the country. The survey resulted in a report that gives special attention to programs that service the hardest-to-reach illiterates.

Publications

The biweekly *CBE Report* contains information about national policies and programs; funding opportunities, workshops, conferences, and publications; and successful programs and practices at the local level. Also published are technical assistance bulletins and special reports, including the findings of the literacy program survey funded by B. Dalton, *Adult Literacy: Study of Community-Based Literacy Programs.*

Sources of Support

Funded initially (1976–81) by the federal government, ACBE has since depended nationally for support on private foundations and corporations. Additional support is provided by membership dues, the sale of publications, and annual conference fees.

40

§20   **Association of American Publishers, Inc. (AAP)**

220 East 23d Street
New York, New York 10010
212-689-8920
Thomas D. McKee, *Senior Vice President*
2005 Massachusetts Avenue, N.W.
Washington, D.C. 20036
202-232-3335
Richard P. Kleeman, *Senior Vice President*
Established in 1970

What/For Whom

The Association of American Publishers represents the United States publishing industry. Its three hundred members are the publishers of the great majority of books and pamphlets sold to American schools, colleges, libraries, bookstores, and, by direct mail, homes. The AAP members also publish scholarly journals and produce a range of educational materials, including maps, films, audio and video tapes, records, slides, test materials, and computer software. AAP membership thus represents a wide spectrum of publishing activity.

The goals of the association are to expand the market for books and other published works, including journals and software; to strengthen public appreciation of the importance of books to the "stability and evolution" of society's values and culture; to provide member houses with information on trade conditions, government policies and attitudes, and other matters of concern to publishers; and to provide programs that can assist members in the management and administration·of their companies. Services include conference, statistical surveys, public information, and press relations.

Examples

1) Freedom to Read Committee. The committee is concerned with protecting freedoms guaranteed by the First Amendment. It analyzes individual cases of attempted censorship and may take action in the form of legal briefs, testimony before appropriate legislative committees, or public statements and telegrams protesting any attempt to limit freedom of communication. It also sponsors public programs and issues periodic educational reports on censorship. For additional information, contact Richard P. Kleeman at the Washington office.

2) International Freedom to Publish Committee. The committee fights for the rights of writers and publishers around the world. For example, the committee provided moral and financial support that enabled the African Writers Association to publish *Classic* magazine. In 1983, it inaugurated a campaign, "Remember the Silenced Writer," to publicize the plight of Soviet writers.

3) The American Book Awards (TABA). The purpose of the awards is to honor and promote books of distinction and literary merit, thereby encouraging reading. Formerly known as the National Book Awards, the awards originated with the Book Manufacturers' Institute (§25). TABA has been under the aegis of AAP since 1980. For further information, contact Barbara Prete at the New York office.

4) A new program at AAP is aimed at eliminating state sales taxes on books in order to encourage book buying and reading. The idea for a national program will be tested first in a brief filed in New York state. For further information, contact Parker Ladd at the New York office.

5) New Technology Committee. The committee launched the Electronic Manuscript Project to develop industry-wide standards and author guidelines for handling manuscripts in electronic format. In 1983–84, the committee sponsored a series of workshops on videodisc technology and held discussions with the Library of Congress regarding its optical digital disk project.

6) "I'd Rather Be Reading." In 1983, the AAP initiated the "I'd Rather Be Reading" promotion campaign. The Center for the Book in the Library of Congress (§30) became the cosponsor in 1984. The slogan appears on various promotional items, such as bumper stickers, buttons, shopping bags, bookmarks, and note pads. For additional information, contact Parker Ladd at the New York office.

Publications *AAP Newsletter,* about eight times a year; *Monthly Report: A News Bulletin for Members of the AAP,* a monthly Washington report.

Sources of Support Membership dues; sale of publications; proceeds from conferences.

§21 Association of American University Presses, Inc. (AAUP)

1 Park Avenue
New York, New York 10016
212-889-6040
Frances Gendlin, *Executive Director*
Established in 1937

What/For Whom AAUP is a service organization of presses that serve as publishing arms of universities and colleges across the United States and in several foreign countries. The association sponsors conferences and seminars that focus on particular phases of university press publishing and help press staff acquire additional skills and knowledge. An annual design competition singles out the outstanding books and jackets of member presses. Through American University Press Services (AUPS), a business subsidiary of AAUP, members are provided with management and marketing services, including an exhibits program that supervises the display of press books at scholarly and professional meetings, and a publications program that issues specialized educational, reference, and professional publications for the scholarly publishing community.

Example

The AUPS Publications Program not only issues publications for the scholarly publishing community, but also serves the library and the general reading community by publishing annual bibliographies of university press books suitable for these other audiences. These bibliographies are prepared in cooperation with professional high school and public library associations. In addition, the program coordinates cooperative advertising space in journals, educational publications, and newspapers, to help scholarly books reach a wider audience.

Publications

The Exchange, a quarterly newsletter; the annual bibliographies *University Press Books for Public Libraries* and *University Press Books for Secondary School Libraries;* various directories.

Sources of Support

Membership dues, conferences, publications, and income from American University Press Services.

---

§22 Authors League of America, Inc., and Authors Guild, Inc.

234 West 44th Street
New York, New York 10036
212-391-9198
Marie Louise Lopez, *Administrator*

What/For Whom

The Authors League of America was founded in 1912 to represent the interests of authors and playwrights regarding copyright, freedom of expression, taxation, and other issues. It consists of two component organizations, the Dramatists Guild and the Authors Guild, Inc. The Authors Guild, Inc., founded in 1921, has focused on the business and professional interests of its members, who are writers of books, poetry, articles, short stories, and other literary works. The guild and the league conduct several symposia each year at which experts provide information on such subjects of interest as privacy and publicity, libel, wills and estates, taxation, copyright, editors and editing, the art of interviewing, and standards of criticism and book reviewing. The league continues to be the sole organization

43

representing authors in ongoing programs of the Copyright Office in the Library of Congress (§53) affecting library photocopying and other major copyright issues. In addition, the Authors League files *amicus curiae* briefs on behalf of writers in the Supreme Court and United States and state appellate courts; testifies before congressional and state legislative committees; and issues public statements on various First Amendment issues, among them secrecy clauses in government contracts and book banning in schools.

Example

In memory of Luise Marie Sillcox, executive sercretary of the Authors League of America for nearly fifty years, the league and the Center for the Book in the Library of Congress have cosponsored two lectures: "The Book," by Barbara W. Tuchman, in 1979, and "The Book Enchained," by Harrison E. Salisbury, in 1983.

Publications

The *Authors Guild Bulletin;* various leaflets and pamphlets.

Sources of Support

Membership dues from the Dramatists Guild and the Authors Guild; activities fees.

---

§23 Bibliographical Society of America

P.O. Box 397, Grand Central Station
New York, New York 10163
718-638-7957
Irene Tichenor, *Executive Secretary*
Established in 1904

What/For Whom

The Bibliographical Society of America promotes bibliographical research and issues a variety of bibliographical publications. It sponsors a fellowship program to encourage bibliographical scholarship. Specific interests include the history of book production, publication, distribution, and collecting, and author bibliography. Membership is open to libraries and individuals interested in bibliographical problems and projects. The Bibliographical Society holds its annual meeting each January in New York City.

Example

The society recently obtained a grant from the H.W. Wilson Foundation for the pilot phase of an archives project to locate and compile a guide to North American manuscript resources in the field of publishing and printing history.

Publications

The quarterly journal *Papers;* occasional monographs, Also, supervision of publication of the ongoing *Bibliography of American Literature.*

Sources of Support

Membership dues, foundation grants, sale of publications.

§24 Book Industry Study Group, Inc. (BISG)

160 Fifth Avenue
New York, New York 10010
212-929-1393
Managing Agent: SKP Associates
Sandra K. Paul, *President*
Established in 1976

What/For Whom

The immediate purpose of the Book Industry Study Group is to promote and support research in and about the industry. BISG is a voluntary, nonprofit research organization composed of individuals and firms from various sectors of the book industry: publishers, manufacturers, suppliers, wholesalers, retailers, librarians, and others engaged professionally in the development, production, and dissemination of books. The group began when the Book Manufacturers' Institute (§25) brought together publishers, manufacturers, and representatives of trade associations to discuss the need to improve the industry's research capability. Trade and professional associations, such as the Association of American Publishers (§20), the Association of American University Presses (§21), and the American Booksellers Association (§8), have joined in this effort to meet the book industry's research and information needs.

Examples

1) *Book Industry Trends* is an annual statistical research report used by the industry in business planning. A monthly supplement, *Trends Update,* provides ongoing information about the industry and explains the forecasting techniques used in preparing the annual report. Both are compiled for BISG under the auspices of the Center for Book Research (§29).

2) BISG prepared two major studies of industry-wide interest: *Book Distribution in the United States* (1982) and the *Consumer Research Study on Reading and Book Purchasing* (1978, updated in 1983), a study of reading and book purchasing patterns among adults, juveniles, and older people. The *Consumer Research Study* and its update were released and discussed at the Center for the Book in the Library of Congress (§30).

3) The Book Industry System Advisory Committee (BISAC) has helped in developing voluntary standardized computer-to-computer communications formats used throughout the industry and in expanding the acceptance of the international standard book number (ISBN) and the standard address number (SAN) within the publishing and bookselling community.

Publications

BISG publishes *Book Industry Study Trends,* annual; the monthly *Trends Update;* and other reports of research.

Sources of Support

Membership dues; sale of publications.

45

§25 Book Manufacturers' Institute, Inc. (BMI)

111 Prospect Street
Stamford, Connecticut 06901
203-324-9670
Douglas E. Horner, *Executive Vice President*
Established in 1933

What/For Whom

BMI is the leading trade association of the book manufacturing industry, and its members manufacture the majority of books published by the U.S. book publishing industry each year. BMI brings together book manufacturers to deal with common concerns and also provides links between book manufacturers and publishers, suppliers, and governmental bodies. BMI conducts studies and programs, collects statistics, and makes forecasts about the industry's future.

Examples

1) Through its affiliation with the Book Industry Study Group, (§24), which it helped to create, BMI has developed a data information program for the industry.

2) The Government Relations Committee and Postal Committee of BMI have worked with their counterparts at the Association of American Publishers (§20) to present the positions of their two industries to various governmental and legislative bodies.

3) With the Association of American Publishers and the National Association of State Textbook Administrators, BMI has developed nationally recognized manufacturing standards for textbooks.

4) Past achievements of BMI include establishment in 1948 of the Bookmobile, an experiment in book marketing now operated by the Association of American Publishers; creation of the National Book Awards, now known as the American Book Awards, also currently administered by the AAP; and establishment of the Library Club of America (1955–61), a reading motivation project aimed at young people.

Source of Support

Membership dues.

§26 Business Council for Effective Literacy (BCEL)

1221 Avenue of the Americas, 35th Floor
New York, New York 10020
212-512-2415
Gail Spangenberg, *Vice President*
Established in 1983

What/For Whom

BCEL is a publicly supported foundation established to foster greater corporate awareness of adult illiteracy and to increase business support and involvement in literacy. BCEL officers and staff work with literacy programs around the country, assessing activities, needs, and problems, in order to advise the business community on the opportunities for their involvement and funding. In addition, the council makes available to the corporate community research reports, professional and technical assistance, and other information services, and sponsors meetings and seminars. It also works with schools, libraries, and other organizations to help develop the additional resources needed to build higher levels of reading competency among children. Harold W. McGraw, Jr. of McGraw-Hill, Inc., founded the council with a personal contribution of $1 million; its Board of Directors includes heads of major corporations and leaders in education and the professions.

Examples

1) Although BCEL does not normally function as a direct grantmaker, in 1984 it made a matching grant to the Coalition for Literacy (§36) to ensure that the Coalition/Advertising Council multimedia National Awareness Campaign for adult literacy would begin on schedule.

2) BCEL is also engaged in a project, which includes a grant to the American Association for Adult and Continuing Education (§5), to examine the resource and funding needs of literacy programs nationwide as they attempt to meet current and future demands for their services as a result of the National Awareness Campaign.

Publications

A quarterly *Newsletter for the Business Community* includes information on corporate literacy activities and on national literacy projects in search of corporate sponsorship. Other publications include a *Directory of Key State Literacy Contacts* and *Turning Illiteracy Around: An Agenda for National Action,* a report that grew out of the BCEL grant to the American Association for Adult and Continuing Education.

Sources of Support

Individual, corporate, and foundation contributions.

§27 Center for Applied Linguistics (CAL)

1118 22d Street, N.W.
Washington, D.C. 20037
202-429-9292
G. Richard Tucker, *President*
Established in 1959

What/For Whom

The Center for Applied Linguistics is a private, nonprofit resource organization engaged in the study of language and the application of linguistics to educational, cultural, and social issues, including literacy, bilingual education, and English as a second or foreign language. Established in 1959 as an autonomous program of the Modern Language Association (§57) and incorporated as an independent organization in 1964, CAL is committed to improving the teaching of English and other languages and to incorporating the findings of the language sciences into social and educational policy, both nationally and internationally. It accomplishes its goals through research; information collection and dissemination; conference sponsorship; technical assistance programs; the development of teaching, testing, and scholarly materials; and participation in formulation of language policy. Its constituency is composed of private and public organizations with an interest in language practice and policy, including congressional offices, news organizations, executive agencies, and state and local officials seeking information and advice in solving language-related problems in a wide variety of contexts.

Examples

1) ERIC Clearinghouse on Languages and Linguistics. The Center for Applied Linguistics operates this ERIC Clearinghouse under a contract from the U.S. Department of Education (§83). The clearinghouse is a comprehensive center for information on bilingualism, bilingual education, and English as a second or foreign language, among other language-related subjects. (See also ERIC Clearinghouse on Reading and Communication Skills [§41].)

2) Meeting the literacy needs of adults and children in the United States and abroad is an important goal of CAL's application of language research to the solution of educational and social problems. Newcomers to the United States, including refugees, immigrants and migrants, are among those whose illiteracy problems are given special attention. CAL conducts research, convenes conferences, generates educational materials illustrating various approaches to literacy, and evaluates reading programs and proposed reading tests, including those being considered for statewide adoption.

Publications

In 1983, CAL merged its publications programs with that of Harcourt Brace Jovanovich, Inc., to expand its audience of

48

scholars and practitioners in the areas of English as a second language and the language sciences more generally. Publications include teaching and scholarly material, including reading-oriented texts and videotapes. One set of materials, for example, deals with the relationship between dialect differences and reading proficiency.

Sources of Support   Federal funds; publications; foundation donations.

---

§28   Center for Book Arts

626 Broadway, 5th Floor
New York, New York 10012
212-460-9768
Robin Siegel, *Executive Director*
Established in 1974

What/For Whom   The Center for Book Arts is a not-for-profit organization whose purpose is to promote and exhibit the art of the book, both historical and contemporary. The center offers lectures, courses, workshops, and exhibitions relating to typography, hand bookbinding, papermaking, letterpress printing, and book production. Book and paper restoration, the construction of boxes and portfolios for conservation, and the history of the book are regularly taught in courses and weekend workshops, while avant-garde creativity in bookmaking is another focus of the center. The center also offers printing and binding services and workshop and studio rental.

Examples   1) The center's list of activities for 1985 included courses in bookbinding, restoration, wood engraving, letterpress printing, and boxmaking and weekend workshops on the clamshell box, paper marbling, and management in alternative publishing.

2) The center organized "One Cubic Foot," a 1983 exhibition at the Metropolitan Museum of Art, for which twelve artists were given a pageless book measuring 12 inches by 12 inches by 1 inch, in which they were allowed to do any artwork, in paper, that they wished, as long as the completed work folded back up into book form.

Publications   The catalog of the center's tenth anniversary exhibition, *The First Decade Catalog*, is available. *Book Arts Review*, a quarterly, includes a national calendar of courses, lectures, etc. on book arts and reviews of books on book arts.

Sources of Support   Membership fees; contributions; grants from foundations, the New York Council on the Arts, and the National Endowment for the Arts.

§29 Center for Book Research

University of Scranton
Scranton, Pennsylvania 18510
717-961-7764
John P. Dessauer, *Director*
Established in 1983

What/For Whom

The Center for Book Research was founded as a department of the University of Scranton to investigate the creation, publication, and use of books, past, present, and future. Research findings are intended both to increase knowledge about the ways in which books serve the educational, cultural, and recreational needs of society and to provide a basis on which investment decisions can be made.

The center sponsors annual conferences on book-related topics of significant public and general interest. Other activities include publication of annual statistical analyses and forecasts, and a quarterly research journal devoted to books.

Examples

1) In 1984, the center held an international conference, "The Book in the Electronic Age."

2) In 1985, the center conducted a survey of library acquisitions practices for the Professional and Scholarly Publishing Division of the Association of American Publishers (§20).

3) The center compiles the statistical study *Book Industry Trends,* published annually, which estimates and forecasts book industry sales in the United States for a ten-year span. The study includes the areas of publishers' and wholesalers' revenues, consumer expenditures, library acquisitions, and publishers' expenditures on book manufacturing. *Book Industry Trends* and its quarterly supplement, *Trends Update,* are published by the Book Industry Study Group (§24).

Publications

As of 1985, *Book Research Quarterly,* which explores the role of the book in contemporary society, including the publishing and book distribution process and the social, political, economic, and technological conditions that help shape it.

Sources of Support

Sponsored research projects and conference funding from various foundations and corporations.

§30

The Center for the Book in the Library of Congress

Washington, D.C. 20540
202-287-5221
John Y. Cole, *Executive Director*
Established in 1977

What/For Whom

The Center for the Book in the Library of Congress was established by an Act of Congress, Public Law 95–129, signed by President Jimmy Carter on October 13, 1977. It was created "to provide a program for investigation of the transmission of human knowledge and to heighten public interest in the role of books and printing in the diffusion of knowledge." This purpose is to be accomplished through such activities as "a visiting scholar program, accompanied by lectures, exhibits, publications, and other related activities."

With help from many advisors, the Center for the Book has developed a program of symposia, projects, and publications concerned with reading promotion, the history of books, the international role of books, and the role of books and reading in contemporary society. Except for basic administrative support provided by the Library of Congress, the Center for the Book is privately financed. Over thirty individuals and sixty-five corporations support its program with tax-deductible contributions. The center views itself as a national catalyst for stimulating public interest in books and reading. Its activities are designed to dramatize the importance of books and reading, to support and strengthen the programs of other organizations in the book and educational communities, and to stimulate research about books and about reading. Two statewide centers have been established with advice and cooperation from the Center for the Book: the Florida Center for the Book, established in Fort Lauderdale in 1984, and the Illinois Center for the Book, in Chicago in 1985. They use private contributions and state and federal grants for reading, book, and library promotion activities. They also help projects inspired by the Center for the Book in the Library of Congress reach a wider audience.

Examples

1) "Read More About It," the CBS Television/Library of Congress book project, is a Center for the Book reading promotion project. Since 1979, over one hundred CBS television presentations have included a thirty-second message, in which the star of the program mentions books suggested by the Library of Congress and sends viewers to their local libraries or bookstores to "Read More About It!"

2) "Books Make a Difference" is a theme developed by the Center for the Book for library and school reading promotion

51

projects. Originating in an oral history project in which people across America were asked, "What book made a difference in your life and what was that difference?" the theme has been especially popular for student essay contests.

3) "A Nation of Readers," another Center for the Book theme, was selected by the American Library Association (§13) as the theme for National Library Week in 1985. On October 16, 1984, in ceremonies at the Library of Congress, the U.S. Postal Service issued a twenty-cent "A Nation of Readers" commemorative stamp. The image on the stamp is President Abraham Lincoln reading to his son Tad.

4) *U.S. Books Abroad: Neglected Ambassadors* (1984), by Curtis G. Benjamin, a study commissioned by the Center for the Book, has been a key document in recent efforts to strengthen the book and library programs of the United States Information Agency (§87).

5) *Books in Our Future* (1984), a report resulting from a year-long study that was authorized by Congress and carried out under the auspices of the Center for the Book, discusses the future of book culture and threats to it.

6) "Books and Other Machines," an exhibition in the Great Hall of the Library of Congress from December 1984 to June 1985, explored the complementary relationships among printed books, technology, and reading.

7) "The Year of the Reader." The Center for the Book has proclaimed 1987 to be "The Year of the Reader" and encourages other organizations to adopt this theme.

Publications

A list of the forty books and pamphlets sponsored by the Center for the Book is available from the center.

Sources of Support

Private funds, with administrative support from the Library of Congress.

§31 Center for the Study of Reading

University of Illinois
51 Gerty Drive, Room 174
Champaign, Illinois 61820
217-333-2552
Jean Osborn, *Associate Director*
Established in 1976

What/For Whom

The Center for the Study of Reading does basic and applied research on the processes that underlie reading, reading comprehension, and how reading skills are acquired. A research staff of thirty-five at the center conducts projects jointly with the Cambridge, Massachusetts, research and development firm of Bolt, Beranek and Newman. The staff brings a variety of perspectives to bear on the study of reading, including scholars in anthropology, computer science, linguistics, literature, and several branches of psychology. The center aims at forming consensus in the American reading community and at communicating warranted conclusions about learning to read in American schools to teachers, parents, authors, publishers, public opinion leaders, and government officials.

Examples

1) Center staff have made about five hundred presentations at professional and scholarly meetings and conducted about two hundred teacher workshops.

2) An estimated eighteen thousand students, from kindergarten through college, have participated in studies performed by the center.

Publications

About fifty Reading Education Reports and three hundred Technical Reports have been prepared and are available through the ERIC system (§83). The center cosponsored the publication of *Becoming a Nation of Readers,* the report of the National Academy of Education's Commission on Reading.

Source of Support

Grants from the U.S. Department of Education (§83).

---

§32 Chicago Book Clinic

664 North Michigan Avenue
Chicago, Illinois 60611
312-951-8254
Trudi Jenny, *President*
Founded in 1936

What/For Whom

The Chicago Book Clinic promotes craftsmanship in the editing and production of books, offers courses in various aspects of publishing, and organizes seminars, lectures, and exhibitions related to publishing and publishing technology. Book Clinic interests extend to commercial, university, and small press publishing. The Book Clinic meets monthly. Its annual exhibit of award-winning designs, one of the most prestigious in the nation, covers textbooks, scholarly books, trade books for adults and children, and other areas. The Chicago Book Clinic draws on a fifteen-state area for its membership.

Examples

1) The Chicago Book Clinic seasonally offers introductory courses in copy editing, book design, and other production areas.

2) The annual exhibit, "Pubtech," is an extensive and well-attended show of new technologies in publishing.

Publications　　　A quarterly, *Jacket Flap,* for members; the catalog of its annual exhibit of award-winning designs.

Sources of Support　　　Membership fees; contributions.

---

§33　　Children's Book Council, Inc. (CBC)

67 Irving Place
New York, New York 10003
212-254-2666
John Donovan, *Executive Director*
Established in 1945

What/For Whom　　　CBC is a nonprofit association of publishers that encourages the reading and enjoyment of children's books. Its members publish children's and young adult trade books—books for independent reading, not textbooks. CBC's best known activity is its annual sponsorship of National Children's Book Week. In addition, in 1984 and 1985 the council sponsored the national conference "Everychild," which featured programming and exhibits designed to increase understanding of how all the media—books, television, movies, magazines, computers and games—educate and provide pleasure to children and young adults.

Besides preparing reading promotion materials, CBC promotes adults' understanding of children's literature and the use of trade books in child-related disciplines. Some of this programming is developed entirely by CBC; some of it through joint CBC committees with such professional organizations as the American Booksellers Association (§8), the American Library Association (§13), the International Reading Association (§51), and the National Council of Teachers of English (§64). CBC does not offer research or marketing advice, but it does make available to the public the resources of its library, including examination copies of books recently published by its members and a professional collection of interest to children's book specialists.

Examples　　　1) American Booksellers Association–Children's Book Council Joint Committee. The committee annually sponsors the exhibit/catalog "Children's Books Mean Business," which brings to booksellers' attention children's books that publishers themselves select as having a special appeal.

2) American Library Association–Children's Book Council Joint Committee. Typical of its ongoing work is "Books for All Ages," a series of pamphlets listing, intermixed, books for young readers and adults.

3) International Reading Association–Children's Book Council Joint Committee. Its project is the annual booklist "Children's Choices: Teaching with Books Children Like."

4) National Council of Teachers of English–Children's Book Council Joint Committee. The committee has prepared a series of articles on "Children's Literature Across the Curriculum," which began to appear in NCTE's journal *Language Arts* in September 1985 and will continue through May 1986.

Publications

The newsletter *CBC Features* (formerly *The Calendar*), irregular, includes information on CBC activities, articles on children's books, and listings of free and inexpensive children's book promotion material available from CBC's publisher members. CBC also administers the preparation of three annual booklists (including lists of children's books in the areas of social studies and science), and produces posters, bookmarks, and other display and promotional material created by well-known children's book illustrators and writers. For adults, the council produces miniseminars on audiocassettes, among them "Reading Black American Poetry and African Folktales" and "Reading Poetry with Children." Occasional reference and informational volumes include the updated bibliographic reference *Children's Books: Awards and Prizes.*

Sources of Support

Publishers' membership dues; the annual conference; sale of materials.

§34   Children's Television Workshop (CTW)

1 Lincoln Plaza
New York, New York 10023
212-595-3456
Keith W. Mielke, *Vice President for Research*
Established in 1968

What/For Whom

Children's Television Workshop is the world's largest independent producer of educational television programs. It uses mass media technologies and techniques to inform and educate preschool children about a variety of subjects, including reading, health, history, science, and technology. Over the years, programming has expanded to include older age groups and foreign languages and cultures. Programs appear on Public Broadcasting System channels (PBS).

A Community Education Services (CES) Division was created in 1969 to develop and sustain target audiences for *Sesame Street* (see below), especially among low-income families and other special viewing groups. Parades, contests, illustrated talks, and house-to-house canvassing of inner-city neighborhoods were used to create awareness of the program and its goals, and special films explaining the educational aims of the program were screened before churches, women's groups, and parent-teacher meetings and at special events. In the mid-1970s, as an outgrowth of these extension efforts, CES specialists began to work with the inmate populations of federal prisons to help maintain and strengthen family ties. In response to the fact that few facilities for visiting children exist at prisons, CES helped to create Sesame Street Centers within the prisons, and equipped them with television sets, toys, children's furniture, and videotape playback machines. CES staff also helped train inmates to run the prison centers, and many prisoners have enrolled in extension courses offered in subjects related to the work of the centers.

Examples

1) *Sesame Street.* Aimed at children under the age of six, *Sesame Street's* curriculum adds cultural and life-style themes to a core of educational basics. Recent emphasis has included print literacy, sound pattern discrimination, prereading, writing, and vocabulary. Celebrity guests have included the first American female astronaut, Sally Ride; jazz performer Cab Calloway; violinist Itzhak Perlman; and actor and singer Harry Belafonte.

2) *The Electric Company.* Designed to help teach certain reading skills to children aged seven to ten, the program is the most widely viewed television series in American classrooms, even though its production ended in 1977. The series pioneered the use of electronic effects, particularly in the placement and movement of print on the screen. As part of its community outreach program, CES developed after-school clubs, called Power Stations, to complement *The Electric Company.* Power Stations organize activities around reading practice and the development of language skills.

Publications

Children's Television Workshop publishes books for prereaders and early readers in cooperation with companies such as Random House and Western Publishing. In addition, the workshop publishes four monthly children's magazines, including *Sesame Street Magazine* and *The Electric Company Magazine,* which employs a news/feature format to encourage youngsters to discover the pleasure of reading. CTW also produces records, toys and games, clothing, and computer software, which incorporates some of the same educational values as the television programs. For adults, CTW commissions special studies of audiences not covered by standard television audience statistics and publishes bibliographies of recent writings on workshop programming and research efforts. *International Research Notes,* published by the workshop's Research Department at irregular intervals, offers information on the research, production, content, and design of CTW programs around the world.

Product licensing royalties; sale of periodicals and records; overseas broadcast fees. Funds for creating new educational television programs are derived from government agencies, public broadcasting sources, foundations, and private corporations.

---

§35 Christian Booksellers Association (CBA)

P.O. Box 200
Colorado Springs, Colorado 80901
303-576-7880
William R. Anderson, *President*
Founded in 1950

What/For Whom

The Christian Booksellers Association is a trade association of religious bookstores. The CBA monitors and compiles statistics on the religious book trade and provides services to members through its publications program, regional meetings, and an annual national convention. The CBA makes awards, provides a placement service, and has some educational activities.

Example

The 1985 CBA convention in Dallas had 8,996 people in attendance, including representatives from over 1,500 member stores.

Publications

A monthly, *Bookstore Journal;* an annual, *Current Christian Books;* an annual directory of suppliers; and a number of manuals useful to member bookstores.

Source of Support

Membership fees.

---

§36 Coalition for Literacy

50 East Huron Street
Chicago, Illinois 60611
312-944-6780
Toll-free literacy hotline: 800-228-8813 (Contact Literacy Center)
Jean Coleman, *Program Officer*
Established in 1981

What/For Whom

Because it felt that a more unified literacy effort was needed to achieve national awareness of the problem of illiteracy, in 1981 the American Library Association (§13) founded the Coalition for Literacy. The coalition consists of eleven organizations that together have organized a massive nationwide attack on adult illiteracy. The three-part, three-year program, headquartered at the American Library Association, began in January 1984.

Part I of the program is a multimillion-dollar National Awareness Campaign in which public service announcements on television, radio, and billboards and in magazines and newspapers alert the public to the magnitude of the illiteracy problem. The advertisements, which publicize the national toll-free telephone number listed above, are also intended to help recruit volunteer program managers, tutors, and corporate sponsors for local literacy efforts, as well as motivate adult illiterates to come forward and ask for help with basic skills. The campaign is cosponsored by the Advertising Council, Inc., with volunteer advertising assistance from member agency Benton & Bowles, Inc.

Part II of the program focuses on the national, toll-free literacy hotline, which provides information on the extent of adult illiteracy and refers callers to local, regional, and state literacy programs for recruitment. The hotline is staffed by the Contact Literacy Center (§37).

Part III of the program offers technical assistance to improve or begin community-based adult literacy projects. In areas from which calls to the toll-free number are numerous but no resources exist, the coalition will help to create new programs.

The coalition's network consists of eleven member organizations that play a role nationally and locally in the delivery of literacy information and services: American Association for Adult and Continuing Education (§5), American Association of Advertising Agencies, American Library Association (§13), B. Dalton Bookseller, Contact Literacy Center, Inc. (§37), International Reading Association (§51), Laubach Literacy Action (§52), Literacy Volunteers of America (§54), National Advisory Council on Adult Education, National Commission on Libraries and Information Science (§62), National Council of State Directors of Adult Education (see §5).

Sources of Support   Membership dues and individual, foundation, and corporate donations. The National Awareness Campaign was started with funds from B. Dalton Bookseller, the U.S. Department of Education (§83), the General Electric Foundation, the New York State Publishers Association, and a matching grant from the Business Council for Effective Literacy (§26).

§37 Contact Literacy Center

P.O. Box 81826
Lincoln, Nebraska 68501-1826
402-464-0602
Toll-free literacy hotline: 800-228-8813
Rhonda Kadavy, *Director of Literacy Services*
Established in 1978

What/For Whom

The Contact Literacy Center is a division of Contact Center, Inc., an international nonprofit organization that offers referral and follow-up services in the areas of criminal justice and human services. The Literacy Center is the information and referral clearinghouse for the Coalition for Literacy (§36), an eleven-member national literacy network. Utilizing a toll-free national hotline (staffed from 8 a.m. to 8 p.m. Monday through Friday, 8 a.m. to 12 noon on Saturday), the center fields inquiries from all over the country resulting from the three-year National Awareness Campaign (see §36) that began in January 1984 as a joint venture of the Coalition for Literacy and the Advertising Council.

The hotline provides information to three main groups. Prospective volunteer tutors receive a listing of literacy programs in their local area and information on how they can become involved. Corporate representatives receive information on how corporations can initiate or support literacy programs. And even through the Advertising Council campaign is not designed to recruit students, those who call are referred to literacy programs in their immediate area. A special cross-referral system, when authorized, enables the Contact Literacy Center to notify area literacy programs of the interest expressed by specific potential tutors, corporations, and students. Referrals can also be provided for adults and children with learning disabilities.

Publications

The Written Word is a monthly newsletter that presents articles on literacy products, programs, and activities around the country. *Reducing Functional Illiteracy: A National Guide to Facilities and Services* is the largest literacy directory available, describing thousands of national, state, local, and grass-roots volunteer literacy programs. It is periodically revised. The center also publishes informational pamphlets on, for example, literacy statistics, fundraising for literacy programs, publicity for literacy programs, how to help your child succeed in reading, how to form a state or local literacy coalition, how to tutor without belonging to an organization, and libraries and literacy.

Sources of Support

Publications; individual, foundation, and corporate donations through the Coalition for Literacy.

59

§38 Council for Basic Education

725 15th Street, N.W.
Washington, D.C. 20005
202-347-4171
Dennis Gray, *Associate Executive Director*
Established in 1956

What/For Whom

Founded by a group of distinguished academic and civic leaders, the Council for Basic Education is a nationwide association of parents, educators, policymakers, and other citizens who advocate strengthening education at the elementary and secondary school level by teaching the basic academic disciplines, which provide what the council sees as basic education. The council further believes that "the first priority of schools should be a sound education in the liberal arts, not just for a favored few, but for all children," thus challenging the idea of a two-track educational system that prepares some students for work and others for college. The ultimate goal is to develop in students the capacity for independent and critical thinking and lifelong learning.

The council promotes its goals in basic education by providing information and analysis of educational research and practice; consulting with schools, school districts, and educational organizations; public speaking; commissioning books and special reports on timely issues; and distributing other publishers' books that it considers important. The emphasis is on primary texts by authors personally engaged in their subjects, rather than on textbooks, workbooks, or edited anthologies. The council is also involved in the teaching of reading in elementary schools. The council has no local or regional affiliates.

Examples

1) Action for Better City Schools. This program focuses public attention on the characteristics of effective schools and helps urban school districts improve the academic achievement of all students.

2) Independent Study in the Humanities. The program offers fellowships for independent summer study to high school teachers of the humanities nationwide. The program was established in 1982 by the council with a grant from the Division of Education Programs of the National Endowment for the Humanities (§67). The aim is to deepen teachers' knowledge of and excitement for subjects closely related to their teaching.

3) Special Programs. The council sponsors some basic education programs that are tailored for local districts.

60

Publications	*Basic Education,* a monthly bulletin; numerous books, reports, and occasional papers; and a series of citizens' guides to aid parents in judging the effectiveness of their local schools.
Sources of Support	Memberships and subscriptions; sale of publications; contributions from individuals and foundations; government grants.

---

§39 Council on Library Resources, Inc. (CLR)

1785 Massachusetts Avenue, N.W.
Washington, D.C. 20036
202-483-7474
Deanna Marcum, *Vice President*
Established in 1956

What/For Whom	The Council on Library Resources is a foundation that helps libraries, particularly academic and research libraries, to make use of emerging technologies to improve operating performance and expand services. CLR interests include, along with advancing technologies, the economics and management of libraries and other information systems. In addition to grants for library management and the professional education and training of librarians, grants are given in the areas of preservation, access, and bibliographic services. The council's program concentrates on academic and research libraries because of their role in collegiate instruction, their centrality to research and scholarship, and what the council regards as "their fundamental importance to society."
Example	The preservation of printed materials has been a continuing interest of CLR. A 1979 council meeting resulted in the formation of the Committee on Production Guidelines for Book Longevity, and in 1983 the council helped fund speakers for a series of conferences on the preservation of library materials, sponsored by the Resources and Technical Services Division of the American Library Association (§13) in cooperation with the Library of Congress. In 1984 the council formed a Preservation Advisory Committee to help guide initial work on a long-term program to preserve the essential holdings of American research libraries. Included is an information program to help improve prospects for public support.
Publications	*Book Longevity,* the 1983 report of the Committee on Production Guidelines for Book Longevity; the quarterly newsletter *CLR Recent Developments.*
Sources of Support	Funding from private foundations and the National Endowment for the Humanities (§67).

§40   Elderhostel, Inc.

80 Boylston Street, Suite 400
Boston, Massachusetts 02116
617-426-7788
Kady Goldfield, *Director of Public Relations*
Established in 1975

What/For Whom

Inspired by the youth hostels and folk schools of Europe, Elderhostel, Inc., is an international, privately supported, non-profit organization that sponsors inexpensive, short-term, residential academic programs for older adults. A network of over seven hundred host institutions, consisting of campuses and historic sites in the United States and abroad, offer courses that usually last one week, are reading-oriented, and concern topics in the liberal arts, sciences, or subjects of local interest. Participants are aged sixty and older or have a participating spouse or companion.

Examples

1) The Elderhostel movement and libraries have been partners on a number of projects. With cooperation from Elderhostel, Inc., New York's Nassau County Library system is sponsoring pilot projects in libraries in Port Washington and Oceanside.

2) American Library Association/Elderhostel Project. Working in cooperation with the American Library Association (§13) and Canadian Library Association, Elderhostel has arranged for special versions of its catalogs to be placed in every public library, both main and branch facilities, in the United States and Canada. Between catalog mailings, libraries receive *Between Classes,* a newsletter that keeps Elderhostelers up to date on the program, as well as brochures, posters, and promotional kits about the program.

Publications

Course catalogs and the newsletter *Between Classes,* both issued three times a year.

Sources of Support

Tuition fees; individual contributions; corporate grants.

§41 ERIC Clearinghouse on Reading and Communication Skills (ERIC/RCS)

National Council of Teachers of English
1111 Kenyon Road
Urbana, Illinois 61801
217-328-3870
Charles Suhor, *Executive Director*
Established in 1966

What/For Whom
The ERIC Clearinghouse on Reading and Communication Skills, housed at the National Council of Teachers of English (§64), is one of sixteen specialized ERIC clearinghouses sponsored by universities or professional associations through contracts with the U.S. Department of Education. The ERIC/RCS center specializes in reading and communication skills, including literacy and children's literature topics. Each clearinghouse collects, evaluates, abstracts, and indexes hard-to-find educational literature; conducts computer searches; commissions studies; and acts as a resource guide. Another ERIC clearinghouse, housed at the Center for Applied Linguistics (§27), specializes in languages and linguistics.

Publications
ERIC/RCS supplies information to the general ERIC publications (§83). In addition, ERIC/RCS prepares minibibliographies of recently added documents that will be useful to the classroom teacher; ERIC/RCS Reports, which appear regularly in a number of journals for educators; *ERIC/RCS News Bulletins,* semiannual newsletters for communication skills educators; and Fact Sheets. ERIC/RCS recently published *Writing Is Reading: 26 Ways to Connect.*

Sources of Support
Federal funds; sales of publications and computer search services; subscriptions.

§42 Freedom to Read Foundation

50 East Huron Street
Chicago, Illinois 60611
312-944-6780
Judith Krug, *Executive Director*
Established in 1969

What/For Whom

The Freedom to Read Foundation consists of librarians, lawyers, booksellers, educators, authors, publishers, and others concerned with preserving the First Amendment rights of freedom of thought and expression. The American Library Association (§13) organized the foundation to support and defend librarians whose positions are jeopardized because of their resistance to abridgements of the First Amendment and to assist in cases that may set legal precedents regarding the freedom of citizens to read. The foundation provides legal and financial assistance to authors, publishers, booksellers, librarians, teachers, students, and others who must go to court to defend this freedom. The foundation reports to the American Library Association on a regular basis on issues of censorship and freedom to read.

Publications

Freedom to Read Foundation News, published quarterly, includes articles and reprints on censorship trends, current court cases, legislative developments in Congress and at the state level, and news regarding battles against censorship by librarians and teachers.

Sources of Support

Membership dues; administrative support from the American Library Association.

§43 Friends of Libraries USA (FOLUSA)

4909 North Ardmore Avenue
Milwaukee, Wisconsin 53217
414-961-2095
Sandy Dolnick, *Executive Director*
Established in 1979

What/For Whom

Friends of Libraries USA is a national organization that works to develop and support local Friends of the Library groups. Members include Friends of Library groups, individuals, libraries, and corporations. FOLUSA is an affiliate of the American Library Association (§13) and holds its meetings in conjunction with ALA's conferences.

Examples	1) Twice a year, during the annual and midwinter ALA conferences, members of FOLUSA meet to share ideas and information.

2) FOLUSA and the Center for the Book in the Library of Congress have held two forums to discuss program ideas for friends groups. |
| **Publications** | *The Friends of Libraries National Notebook,* quarterly, includes program ideas, materials to sell or buy, and news of other friends groups throughout the country. A directory of friends groups is being compiled. |
| **Sources of Support** | Membership dues; corporate support; sale of publications; administrative support from the American Library Association. |

---

§44   Great Books Foundation (GBF)

40 East Huron Street
Chicago, Illinois 60611
312-332-5870
Richard P. Dennis, *President*
Founded in 1947

What/For Whom	The Great Books Foundation, claiming 390,000 members, supports discussion groups on classic books for adults and children throughout the United States. At present, five newly developed series of titles for adults and series for second through twelfth grades are available; five further series for adults will be available within a few years. Each year, GBF trains about 16,000 discussion leaders in two-day sessions that are held in all fifty states. Discussion groups meet every couple of weeks for adults and at various intervals for children. Until the 1970s, most discussion groups met in public libraries; now, most groups meet in local schools. Titles discussed include ancient and modern classics of literature, philosophy, and other areas.
Example	Adult Series B includes works from Freud, Dostoyevsky, Mann, Aeschylus, Thucydides, Aristophanes, Aquinas, Rousseau, Kant, Voltaire, Aristotle, Shakespeare, the Old Testament, Gibbon, Nietzsche, and Shaw.
Publications	GBF publishes the series of paperback books used in Great Books discussion groups.
Sources of Support	Training fees; sales of books.

§45 Guild of Book Workers

521 Fifth Avenue
New York, New York 10175
212-757-6454
Caroline F. Schimmel, *President*
Founded in 1906

What/For Whom	The Guild of Book Workers promotes quality in the hand book crafts: bookbinding, calligraphy, illumination, and decorative papermaking. The guild sponsors exhibitions and offers lectures, workshops, and discussion groups.
Example	In Spring 1985, the guild sponsored workshops on hand bookbinding, Danish bookbinding, "Photographing Your Work," and marbling in New York, Washington, and San Francisco.
Publications	A quarterly newsletter and a semiannual journal.
Sources of Support	Membership fees; workshop fees.

§46 Information Industry Association (IIA)

316 Pennsylvania Avenue, S.E., Suite 400
Washington, D.C. 20003
202-544-1969
Paul G. Zurkowski, *President*
Founded in 1968

What/For Whom	The Information Industry Association is composed of for-profit information companies and information professionals. Many members are publishers of reference books and serials, and IIA has a strong interest in the electronic delivery of information. IIA's workshops, seminars, and publications introduce members to business practices and technologies that will help to identify information needs and to deliver information cost-effectively to customers. IIA's Public Policy and Government Relations Council responds to the effects on information firms of government actions, frames policies for adoption by IIA, and testifies before various government agencies.
Example	In 1983, the Nielsen Company surveyed the United States information industry for the IIA. The survey's results reveal, for example, that almost thirty percent of the 1982 information revenue of the industry came from sale of computerized information.

| Publications | *Friday Memo,* weekly; *Information on Washington,* a monthly report on legislation, administrative actions, court cases, and federal studies that affect the information industry; *Information Times,* three times a year; a descriptive membership directory; surveys and proceedings. |

| Sources of Support | Membership fees; revenues from activities and publications. |

§47 International Board on Books for Young People (IBBY)

Leonhardsgraben 38a
CH-4051, Basel
Switzerland
41-6125-3404
Leena Maissen, *Executive Secretary*
Founded in 1953

United States Board on Books for Young People, Inc. (USBBY)

c/o International Reading Association
800 Barksdale Road, P.O. Box 8139
Newark, Delaware 19714-8139
302-731-1600
Alida von Krogh Cutts, *Executive Secretary*
U.S. National Section of IBBY founded in 1958
USBBY formed in 1984

| What/For Whom | The International Board on Books for Young People promotes international understanding through children's books. It encourages high standards for children's books, translations of children's books, the establishment of public and school libraries, and the use of literature in education. The biennial congresses of IBBY have focused on such topics as books and illustrations, books and the school, and children's literature and the developing countries. IBBY gives a prestigious award in writing and illustrating books for children. IBBY serves as an advisor to national and international groups and has consultative relations with UNICEF and Unesco.

The United States Board on Books for Young People is one of about forty national sections of IBBY. It encourages the provision of reading materials of merit to young people throughout |

the world and cooperates with IBBY and similar organizations. USBBY pays United States dues to IBBY and attempts to give money to IBBY beyond those dues. USBBY was formed in 1984 from two existing groups, the U.S. National Section of IBBY and Friends of IBBY, Inc. The American Library Association (§13) and the Children's Book Council (§33) are charter patron members of USBBY; other members are dues-paying individuals, organizations, businesses, and foundations.

Examples	1) The Hans Christian Andersen Medal for children's authors and illustrators, created by IBBY and awarded annually, is often called the "Little Nobel Prize."
	2) An IBBY exhibition, "Books and Disabled Children," created in 1981, is touring the world.
Publications	IBBY's publication of record, *Bookbird*, published three times a year; a semiannual newsletter from USBBY.
Sources of Funding	For both IBBY and USBBY, membership fees and contributions.

§48 International Book Committee (IBC)

c/o International Reading Association
701 Dallam Road
Newark, Delaware 19711
Ralph Staiger, *Chairman*
Founded in 1972

What/For Whom	The International Book Committee is a committee of representatives of international organizations from throughout the book field; for example, the International Federation of Library Associations and Institutions (§49), International PEN (see §72), and the International Reading Association (§51) are among IBC's sixteen member organizations. IBC was formed as an outgrowth of the 1972 International Book Year support committee and was fundamental in the formulation of the declaration, "Towards a Reading Society," adopted by the 1982 World Congress on Books. Reorganized in 1984, IBC is currently aimed at fostering the creating of a reading environment in all types and at all levels of society, one of the targets set by the 1982 world congress. IBC consults with Unesco on book matters and makes recommendations to governments and non-governmental organizations. IBC awards the International Book Award for outstanding services rendered to the cause of books.
Sources of Support	Member organizations may sponsor delegates to meetings of the IBC.

§49 International Federation of Library Associations and Institutions (IFLA)

c/o Koninklijke Bibliotheek
Prins Willem Alexanderhof 5
The Hague, Netherlands
070-140884
Margreet Wijnstroom, *Secretary General*
Founded in 1927

What/For Whom

IFLA promotes international cooperation and development in librarianship and bibliography. IFLA is an association of national library associations and other library institutions, such as libraries, library schools, and bibliographic institutes—associations, on one hand, and institutions, on the other, have slightly different rights within IFLA. IFLA's strongest programs are in the areas of universal bibliographic control, universal availability of publications, and standards for computerized cataloging. IFLA also devotes concentrated attention to third-world library development by involving third-world librarians in IFLA, sponsoring projects like an investigation of how to catalog African authors' names, and preparing curricula for training librarians in developing countries. IFLA has granted consultative status to a number of international organizations concerned with documentation and librarianship.

Examples

1) The Universal Bibliographic Control program promulgates international bibliographic standards and encourages the production of national bibliographies.

2) The Universal Availability of Publications program facilities international access to harder-to-obtain publications. It promotes national and international lending programs.

3) The International MARC program aims at standardizing the computerized cataloging of books and other materials.

Publications

IFLA Journal and *International Cataloguing* are quarterlies; IFLA is also responsible for two monographic series.

Sources of Support

Funding from Unesco, the Council on Library Resources, and national libraries; membership fees.

§50 International Publishing Association (IPA)

3 Avenue de Miremont
CH-1206 Geneva
Switzerland
022-463018
J. Alexis Koutchoumow, *Secretary-General*
Established in 1896

What/For Whom   The International Publishing Association is a nongovernmental, international, organization of national publishing associations. It holds a congress every four years to discuss current issues affecting the international book trade, publishing, copyright, and related matters.

Example   The twenty-second IPA Congress, held in Mexico City in 1984, drew six hundred delegates. The principal discussion topics were new technologies and their effects on publishing, international copyright, and censorship and the freedom to publish.

Publications   *IPA Publishing News*, and monographs such as *Freedom to Publish (La Liberté de Publication)* by Peter Calvocoressi, and *Roadmap for the Electronic Publisher*, by J. Kist.

Source of Support   Membership dues.

§51 International Reading Association (IRA)

800 Barksdale Road, P.O. Box 8139
Newark, Delaware 19714-8139
302-731-1600
Ronald Mitchell, *Executive Director*
Established in 1956

What/For Whom   The International Reading Association is a nonprofit, professional organization of classroom teachers, reading specialists, administrators, educators of reading teachers, reading researchers, parents, librarians, psychologists, and others interested in improving reading instruction. In 1985 it had over fifty thousand members. IRA encourages study of the reading process, research, and better teacher education; sponsors conferences; and promotes recognition of the importance of reading, skill in reading, and the development of a lifetime reading habit. Volunteer committees of IRA explore such subjects as computer technology and reading, early childhood and literacy

70

development, intellectual freedom, parents and reading, reading and literacy, the impact of court decisions on reading, and adult literacy.

Examples

1) The International Reading Association is one of eleven organizations in the Coalition for Literacy (§36), which is dedicated to eradicating adult illiteracy in the United States, beginning with a three-year, multimedia National Awareness Campaign supported by a national literacy hotline.

2) International Reading Association Literacy Award. IRA regularly honors outstanding achievement in fields relating to reading and reading education. Among them is the IRA Literacy Award, presented by Unesco on International Literacy Day each year for outstanding work in the promotion of literacy.

3) Celebrate Literacy. This second IRA literacy award program takes place at the local level. Participating local councils identify and, through an awards ceremony, recognize a local individual, agency, or institution for significant contributions to literacy.

4) IRA also makes other awards for teaching, service to the profession, research, media coverage of reading, and children's book writing. Among them are the Broadcast Media Awards for Radio and Television, which recognize outstanding reporting and programming on radio, television, and cable television that deals with reading and literacy.

5) Reading and the Aging. This Special Interest Group affiliated with the IRA holds meetings at the IRA annual conference and solicits articles, which it publishes in its newsletter. For further information, contact Claire V. Sibold, Editor, 8337 East San Salvador Drive, Scottsdale, Arizona 85258.

6) Newspaper in Education Week, cosponsored annually by the IRA and the American Newspaper Publishers Association Foundation (§14), focuses on using newspapers to teach young people to read.

Publications

IRA's four professional journals are *The Reading Teacher,* for elementary school educators; *Journal of Reading,* for those concerned with the teaching of reading at secondary, college, and adult levels; *Reading Research Quarterly,* a technical journal for those interested in reading research; and *Lectura y Vida* ("Reading and Life"), published quarterly in Spanish by the Latin American office in Buenos Aires, Argentina. The bimonthly newspaper *Reading Today* contains news and features about the reading profession. Other publications include reports, bibliographies, critical collections, and other aids for the teacher, some in Spanish.

Sources of Support

Membership dues; publications, advertising, and activities fees. Funds from private and governmental agencies are only for special projects.

§52   Laubach Literacy Action (LLA)

1320 Jamesville Avenue, Box 131
Syracuse, New York 13210
315-422-9121
Peter A. Waite, *Executive Director*
Established in 1955

What/For Whom

One of the nation's largest volunteer organizations, Laubach Literacy Action is the United States arm of Laubach Literacy International. LLA combats adult and adolescent illiteracy nationwide by providing basic literacy instruction and English instruction for speakers of other languages, training tutors, publishing educational materials for students and tutors, providing referral services, and disseminating information on literacy. Its network of over fifty thousand volunteers provides tutoring to adult illiterates in forty-six states. Laubach uses its own textbooks and one-on-one method of literacy instruction. Nonreaders and low–reading-level adults not reached by other programs are special concerns of LLA. In addition to promoting adult literacy nationally, LLA has programs that work with community agencies, including public adult education agencies, social service organizations, churches, service clubs, libraries, and prisons. Volunteers are trained both to tutor and to administer programs.

Examples

1) Laubach has joined ten other literacy and educational organizations in a National Awareness Campaign against illiteracy. Among the eleven organizations that have mobilized in this Coalition for Literacy (§36), Laubach is particularly well equipped to meet the demand for training and technical assistance arising from the campaign because of the size of the volunteer network it has available to do actual tutoring.

2) Laubach sponsor Barbara Bush (wife of Vice President George Bush) is donating the proceeds from her new book, *C. Fred's Story,* to advance literacy efforts by LLA and Literacy Volunteers of America (§54).

3) To honor the one hundredth birthday of Dr. Frank C. Laubach, a pioneer of world literacy, the U.S. Post Office issued a 30-cent commemorative stamp on September 2, 1984.

4) Laubach Literacy Action is working with B. Dalton Bookseller to expand literacy services in target sites throughout the United States. Local B. Dalton stores provide volunteers, administrative expertise, and promotional assistance, while Laubach staff assess local literacy needs and develop long-range plans to meet those needs.

5) LLA has been working with Literacy Volunteers of America (§54) and the federal agency ACTION (§1) to develop administrative training for volunteer leaders of local literacy projects.

Publications

New Readers Press, Laubach Literacy International's United States publishing division, produces teaching and tutor-training materials aimed at "new readers" in community-based literacy programs. The press also publishes a weekly newspaper, *News for You,* as well as leisure books written for adults and older youth whose reading skills are at sixth grade-level or lower.

Sources of Support

Individual contributions; membership dues; publications income; donations from corporations and foundations.

---

§53 Library of Congress

Washington, D.C. 20540
202-287-5000
Established in 1800

What/For Whom

The Library of Congress, the world's largest library, contains more than 20 million books and millions of maps, manuscripts, periodicals, films, recordings, prints, and photographs. It has more than 5,500 employees. Although benefiting from deposits to the Copyright Office, which is one of its departments, the Library of Congress does not contain a copy of every book printed in the United States. Nevertheless, by the end of its 1984 fiscal year, the library's collections numbered 81,905,061 items. It is an international library, for it maintains acquisitions offices outside the United States, catalogs books in over 450 languages, and exchanges publications with institutions around the world. It is estimated that two-thirds of the publications currently received by the Library of Congress are in languages other than English.

The Library of Congress is part of the legislative branch of the government. It is both the legislative library for the Congress and "the nation's library," serving readers and researchers not only in Washington but throughout the United States. Library of Congress offices with specialized interests in the creation, preservation, and use of books and in stimulating public interest in books and reading include the Copyright Office, the Preservation Office, the Cataloging-in-Publication Office, the Research Services Department, the National Library for the Blind and Physically Handicapped, the Children's Literature Center, and the Center for the Book (§30).

Examples

1) At the request of Congress, the Copyright Office, which administers the laws protecting the creative works of U.S. citizens, sponsored a symposium on the effects of new technologies on copyright law.

73

2) In fiscal year 1984, Congress appropriated $11.5 million for construction of a unique book preservation facility in nearby Frederick, Maryland. This new Library of Congress facility will permit treatment of hundreds of thousands of books each year through mass deacidification, a new solution to the severe problem of deteriorating book paper.

3) In 1984 the National Library Service for the Blind and Physically Handicapped produced and distributed the first cassette-recorded edition of the Houghton Mifflin Company's *Concise Heritage Dictionary*. This edition uses voice indexing techniques to help readers locate entries.

4) The Geography and Map Division, in cooperation with the Center for the Book, sponsored a 1984 international symposium about atlases both as books and as influences in society, "Images of the World: The Atlas Through History." A major exhibition on the same topic was mounted by the library's Exhibits Office.

5) A November 1984 symposium, "Stepping Away from Tradition: Children's Books of the Twenties and the Thirties," sponsored by the Children's Literature Center and the Center for the Book, focused on the design, publishing, and reading of children's books. A 1985 symposium was on "Collecting Children's Books."

6) *The Early Illustrated Book: Essays in Honor of Lessing J. Rosenwald* (1982) is based on scholarly papers commissioned by the Center for the Book for a symposium sponsored with the Rare Book and Special Collections Division.

Publications

Library of Congress Publications in Print 1985, available without charge from the Library's Central Services Division, lists 656 books, pamphlets, and serials, sixty-three folk and music recordings, and thirty-one literary recordings.

Sources of Support

Federal government, supplemented by gift and trust funds.

§54 Literacy Volunteers of America (LVA)

404 Oak Street
Syracuse, New York 13203-2994
315-474-7039
Jinx Crouch, *Executive Director*
Founded in 1962

What/For Whom

LVA's national organization combats adult illiteracy through a network of local affiliates that offer training and support for community volunteer literacy programs. LVA has over two hundred chapters in thirty-one states. More than thirty thousand tutors and students are involved in its programs. One-on-one instruction is offered in both basic literacy and English as a second language. Unlike Laubach Literacy Action (§52), Literacy Volunteers of America recommends no single method or series of textbooks. The major emphasis in publication is on the development of training materials for program administrators, trainers, and tutors. LVA also provides technical assistance to beginning programs, disseminates literacy information, and provides referral services to potential tutors and students.

Examples

1) LVA is one of the eleven members of the Coalition for Literacy (§36).

2) Literacy Volunteers of America and Laubach Literacy Action, funded jointly by B. Dalton Bookseller and ACTION (§1), developed a management system for establishing literacy programs in new communities.

3) Wally Amos, LVA's national spokesman, who is known for his "literacy awareness events," donated 5 percent of the royalties from his new autobiography, *The Face That Launched a Thousand Chips,* and arranged for a portion of the profits from his new Beatrice Foods product, Louis Sherry/Famous Amos Chocolate Chip Cookie Ice Cream, to support the work of LVA.

4) Celebrity promotion. Shirley MacLaine gave a benefit performance for Literacy Volunteers of New York City.

5) Reader's Digest Foundation gave LVA a grant to make core libraries of teaching materials available to new affiliates and their volunteer tutors.

6) Video adaptations of the Basic Reading Tutor Training Workshop, financed by public and private funds, enable LVA to train more tutors in remote areas.

7) In conjunction with the Gannett Foundation, LVA created a curriculum and training guide for using newspapers to teach reading.

Publications

With a grant from B. Dalton Bookseller, LVA recently revised its *Management Handbook for Volunteer Programs,* which offers practical guidelines to organizations for establishing and operating literacy programs, either as components of an existing agency or as independent affiliates. LVA also publishes the newsletter *The Reader* and a series of leisure books for beginning adult readers, developed under a grant from the National Endowment for the Humanities (§67).

Sources of Support

Sale of training and support materials; membership fees; fees for technical assistance to non-member organizations; trust funds; government agency funding for projects; contributions from foundations, corporations, and individuals.

§55 Lutheran Church Women — Volunteer Reading Aides Program (VRA)

2900 Queen Lane
Philadelphia, Pennsylvania 19129
215-438-2200
Martha A. Lane, *Coordinator*
Established in 1969

What/For Whom

The country's largest church-sponsored adult literacy program, the Lutheran Church Women's Volunteer Reading Aides Program trains volunteer tutors and organizes community-based literacy programs where none already exists. Nonmembers of the Lutheran Church are welcome both as tutors and students. The VRA program also conducts literacy workshops for libraries and community agencies and provides literacy referral and general information services to the Lutheran Church in America and the general public.

Examples

1) Through VRA, the Lutheran Church Women offer training to professional teachers in the principles of teaching English to speakers of other languages (ESOL).

2) The VRA program has helped migrant and native Canadian groups select and write materials suited to specialized literacy needs.

Publications

The VRA program develops and publishes inexpensive, easy-to-read materials for new readers and ESOL students, and resource materials for tutors and literacy program leaders.

Sources of Support

Donations from Lutheran Church Women and other church members; sale of publications, films, and videotapes; service fees from groups requesting assistance.

§56   Minnesota Center for Book Arts (MCBA)

24 North 3d Street
Minneapolis, Minnesota 55401
612-338-3634
Jim Sitter, *Executive Director*
Founded in 1985

What/For Whom

The Minnesota Center for Book Arts preserves and promotes the book arts, concentrating on hand arts, and educates the public about their aesthetic, social, historic, and commercial aspects. MCBA is a working museum of letterpress printing, hand bookbinding, and hand papermaking. Its workshops are open for tours and classes and available for rental by craftsmen. MCBA also organizes exhibitions and lectures and cooperates with other local institutions that are concerned with graphic arts, rare books, and the history of the book.

Examples

1) MCBA offers classes in papermaking, printing, and binding.

2) MCBA, together with several other local organizations, sponsored a lecture by David Godine, "The Future of the Common Book," in May 1985.

Sources of Support

Gifts from local and national corporations and foundations and from individuals; membership fees.

§57   Modern Language Association of American (MLA)

62 Fifth Avenue
New York, New York 10011
212-741-7871
Hans Rutimann, *Deputy Executive Director*
Established in 1883

What/For Whom

The largest organization of academic professionals in the United States, the MLA is devoted to the study and teaching of liberature, languages, and linguistics. Its members are teachers, graduate students, journalists, librarians, administrators, poets, novelists, editors, translators, and other interested professionals, including independent scholars. The MLA provides leadership to the profession in curriculum, teaching, and faculty development through conferences and workshops in its English and foreign language programs. It educates its members in the developments and uses of new technology through publications and programs. It advocates the study of language and literature and the cause of the humanities to Congress, federal agencies, state and local governments, and the media.

MLA divisions encompass various time periods of English, American, and foreign-language literatures and varying approaches for studying them. among them Language and Society; Philosophical Approaches to Literature, including the History of Ideas; and Children's Literature. Discussion groups are designed to accommodate the scholarly and professional interests of smaller constituencies within the organization. They focus, for example, on autobiography, biography, and lexicography.

Example

MLA Committee on Academic Freedom. The committee takes action on censorship and freedom of expression issues both within and outside of academe through public statements and the filing of amicus curiae briefs. For example, the committee opposes restrictions on books and instructional approaches and speaks out against threats to teachers' freedom of speech and employment.

Publications

The *MLA Newsletter,* quarterly, supplies information about the association and the profession. The journal *PMLA,* six times a year, contains articles on scholarship and teaching. *Profession,* an annual anthology, publishes articles on professional and pedagogical topics. The *ADE* (Association of Departments of English) *Bulletin* and The *ADFL* (Association of Departments of Foreign Languages) *Bulletin* publish articles on professional, pedagogical, curricular, and departmental issues of concern to the profession as a whole. The MLA prepares and publishes many other publications.

Sources of Support

Membership dues; sale of publications; proceeds from conferences; Career Information Service fees; and sale of computer services.

§58   National Adult Education Clearinghouse (NAEC)

Center of Adult Continuing Education
Montclair State College
Upper Montclair, New Jersey 07043
201-893-4353
Frances M. Spinelli, *Director*
Established in 1970

What/For Whom

The National Adult Education Clearinghouse provides instructional materials and information about adult continuing education, primarily to college and university libraries, organizations, and government officials. It maintains a twenty-five-thousand-volume lending and mail loan library. There are special collections in various areas, among them, adult continuing education training materials for professionals, paraprofessionals and volunteers; aging; adult learners with disabilities; basic skills, including reading; and English as a second language. NAEC also provides computer search services and on-site materials workshops.

Publications
Adult Education Clearinghouse Newsletter, monthly; monographs; and instructional materials for readers at all levels.

Sources of Support
Sale of publications; subscriptions to the newsletter; computer search services.

---

§59 National Association of College Stores (NACS)

528 East Lorain Street
Oberlin, Ohio 44074
216-775-7777
Garis F. Distelhorst, *Executive Director*
Established in 1923

What/For Whom
NACS is a trade association of retail stores that sell books, supplies, and other merchandise to students and faculties of educational institutions. Members also include publishers and suppliers to the college store market. The association was established to educate and aid college stores in achieving professional, profitable operation; to encourage open involvement and cooperation with college administration, faculty, students, and the community at large; and, to promote greater awareness of college stores, educational and financial contributions to their schools. Though the association is nonprofit, it manages NACSCORP, a member-service, for-profit subsidiary that distributes books, computer software, calendars, and student-rate magazine subscription cards. NACS also conducts one-week professional management seminars throughout the year for college store managers and sponsors an annual Trade Fair that is the industry's only trade show.

Examples
1) NACS promotes reading to the college market by encouraging member stores to do book promotions in conjunction with the American Booksellers Association's Banned Books Campaign (§8). NACS also contributes to Reading Is Fundamental (§75), which focuses on children from the age of three through the high school years.

2) *Reading Rainbow* productions (§76). NACS funds help support this PBS series designed to motivate children to read through programs that feature children's books, animation, and the use of guest narrators.

3) "Robert Kennedy and His Times." NACS launched a major promotion contest for this 1985 television program, in cooperation with the CBS Television/Library of Congress "Read More About It" book project, administered by the Center for the Book in the Library of Congress (§30). The winning store manager received a trip to Washington, D.C.

Publications

The College Store Journal is a trade magazine issued six times a year. The *College Store Buyers' Guide, Book Buyers' Manual,* and *NACS Weekly Bulletin* keep members informed of developments and activities in the industry and the association and among members. Featured regularly in the *Bulletin* is an account of what books are being read on campus, based upon a tabulation compiled by *The Chronicle of Higher Education,* with comparable positions shown for *The New York Times* and *Publishers Weekly* listings.

Sources of Support

Membership dues; seminar fees; sale of publications; NACSCORP operations.

---

§60 National Book Critics Circle (NBCC)

c/o Newsday
Long Island, New York 11747
Brigitte Weeks, *President*
Founded in 1974

What/For Whom

The National Book Critics Circle is a national professional association of book critics and book review editors. NBCC has about 480 members. It aims at elevating standards of book reviewing, promoting public awareness of good book criticism, and improving communication between publishers and reviewers.

Examples

1) The annual presentation of awards in biography, criticism, fiction, nonfiction, and poetry is the best known NBCC program.

2) In 1985, NBCC launched a campaign to encourage publishers to name reviewers, not just newspapers, when quoting reviews for jacket, flap, or advertising copy and to encourage publishers to be more scrupulous in excerpting quotations for such copy.

Publication

A quarterly journal.

Source of Support

Membership fees.

§61 National Coalition Against Censorship (NCAC)

132 West 43d Street
New York, New York 10036
212-944-9899
Leanne Katz, *Executive Director*
Established in 1974

What/For Whom

NCAC is an alliance of national organizations, including religious, educational, professional, artistic, labor, and civil rights groups, committed to defending freedom of thought, inquiry, and expression. The coalition educates its own members about the dangers of censorship and how to oppose them and uses the mass media to inform the general public about censorship issues. Other coalition activities include conferences, program assistance, advocacy, and the monitoring of legislation with First Amendment implications at both national and state levels. NCAC compiles and disseminates educational material, including information packets on many First Amendment-related issues, among them creationism, women and pornography, guidelines for selecting educational materials, government secrecy, and censorship and black literature.

Example

NCAC's Clearinghouse on School Book-Banning Litigation collects and makes available to librarians, journalists, lawyers, educators, school boards, parents, and the public at large up-to-date information on the status of school censorship cases and appropriate legal documents.

Publications

The quarterly newsletter *Censorship News;* periodic reports and background papers; and *Books on Trial: A Survey of Recent Cases,* a source of information on litigation arising from censorship in private schools in the United States, with a listing of books, magazines, and films involved. *Books on Trial* complements NCAC's earlier publication, *Report on Book Censorship Litigation in Public Schools.*

Sources of Support

Individual contributions; sale of publications; conference fees; grants.

§62 National Commission on Libraries and Information Science (NCLIS)

General Services Administration Building
7th and D Streets, S.W., Suite 3122
Washington, D.C. 20024
202-382-0840
Toni Carbo Bearman, *Executive Director*
Established in 1970

What/For Whom

NCLIS is a permanent, independent agency of the United States government, established by Public Law 91–345 to advise the president and Congress on library and information policies and plans in order to meet the needs of all United States citizens. In its second decade, NCLIS program objectives center on the library and information needs of special constituencies, such as cultural minorities, the elderly, and rural Americans. The commission believes that its goal of equal access to library and information services for all citizens implies universal literacy and therefore works with members of the library and information community and various agencies of the executive branch on literacy programs. Another focus of NCLIS is the new technologies and their applications to the library and information field.

Examples

1) Task Force on Library and Information Services to Cultural Minorities. As part of its program to identify users of library and information services and their changing needs, the commission recently reported on the interests and needs of four minority groups, whose members will constitute over one-third of the United States population by the year 2025: black; hispanic; Asian and Pacific Islander; and American Indian, Eskimo, and Aleut.

2) Services to the Elderly. NCLIS is investigating the library and information needs of older Americans and the current availability of library and information services to them. The results of the study will be used to recommend new policies and follow-up action. Interagency cooperation on this project comes from the Administration on Aging, the American Library Association (§13), the Chief Officers of State Library Agencies, the American Association of Retired Persons (§6), the Alliance of Information and Referral Systems, the National Association of State Units on Aging, the National Association of Area Agencies on Aging, the National Council on the Aging (§65), and other professional groups.

3) National Rural Information Services Development Program. The focus of this program is on improving the delivery of library and information services to rural citizens. Under this program, the rural library will take on the role of a comprehensive community learning/information center that uses the latest computer and telecommunications technologies. Functioning as a catalyst in this cooperative program, NCLIS works closely with the library and information community, the U.S. Department of Agriculture, the cooperative extension services, and the nation's state universities and land-grant colleges.

4) Literacy activity. The commission advises the Department of Education (§83) in its coordination of the Adult Literacy Initiative (§84) and is one of eleven literacy and education organizations that constitute the Coalition for Literacy (§36). Another effort to promote literacy, the U.S. Army/NCLIS Reading Project, coordinated with the Department of Defense, is designed to transfer technology developed to increase reading skills in the military to library-based literacy programs.

5) The commission recently completed a unique public/ private sector project in cooperation with the International Business Machines Corporation (IBM) on "U.S. Population Characteristics and Implications for Library and Information Services." The study emphasizes how changing demographic patterns for rural residents, older people, and the nations's four largest cultural minorities will create new demands for library and information services and alter traditional patterns of support for libraries.

Publications   Task force reports; articles; special publications, including the report of the Task Force on Library and Information Services to Cultural Minorities.

Source of Support   Federal government.

---

§63 National Council for Families and Television (NCFT)

20 Nassau Street, Suite 200
Princeton, New Jersey 08542
609-921-3639
Nicholas B. Van Dyck, *President*
Established in 1977

What/For Whom   The National Council for Families and Television is committed to strengthening television's role as an informal educator. To enhance the quality of television programming, it promotes the exchange of information among children, parents, teachers, child development experts, and producers and distributors of television programming, especially prime-time series, specials, and movies of the week. The council also works with teachers and parents to improve children's ability to use what they see on commercial television to enhance learning in school. Council members include television industry and programming executives, producers, writers, directors, network broadcasters, and advertisers; industry grantmaking specialists; scholars, professional educators, and child development specialists; and the National PTA (§69).

To enhance the quality, interest, and informational accuracy of television programming for children, teens, and their families, the council schedules seminars, lecture series, and conferences for scholars and industry professionals. Conferences and workshops aimed at the industry have been conducted on topics such as drug abuse, alcohol, television violence, human sexuality, ethnic stereotyping, and books and reading. Formerly known as the National Council for Children and Television, the organization recently changed its name to reflect its conviction that the role television plays in the lives of children and teenagers needs to be seen in the context of the entire family.

Example

NCFT Teachers Workshops. The council develops, field-tests, and provides hands-on training in teaching methods that improve students' skills in reading, writing, critical thinking, science, math, and social studies by capitalizing on their interest in prime-time television entertainment and information programming. One such workshop was titled "Television Viewing and Reading." Workshops are presented in cooperation with regional and national educational associations.

Publications

Television & Children, quarterly, is a forum for information, research, and opinion. *NCFT Information Service,* monthly, includes news, features, research abstracts, and reprinted articles aimed at television writers, story developers, producers, and programming executives. NCFT Teachers Workshop teaching strategies have been made available to a larger group of teachers and students through the distribution of one hundred thousand teachers' guides and classroom posters in cooperation with Boys Town, the American Academy of Pediatrics, the American Psychological Association, and the National PTA.

Sources of Support

Contributions from individuals, corporations, and foundations.

§64

National Council of Teachers of English (NCTE)

1111 Kenyon Road
Urbana, Illinois 61801
217-328-3870
L. Jane Christensen, *Associate Executive Director*
Established in 1911

What/For Whom

NCTE is a nonprofit professsional service organization committed to improving the teaching of literature and the English language. It emphasizes the need to teach English as both a system of language skills and a humane discipline. Most of NCTE's ninety thousand members are English teachers, teacher educators, and researchers.

The NCTE provides information on the teaching of English and sponsors conferences and two major conventions annually. Committees and task forces conduct and encourage research on topics including composition, media, and reading. Liaison committees carry out projects with other professional groups, among them, the Children's Book Council (§33) and the International Reading Association (§51).

Examples

1) ERIC Clearinghouse on Reading and Communication Skills (§41). NCTE operates the center under a federal contract from the U.S. Department of Education's National Institute of Education. The clearinghouse is a computerized database center for information on all kinds of educational literature.

2) NCTE has collaborated with the International Reading Association on a statement warning against the use of unreliable readability formulas for textbooks to determine what children can and should read.

3) NCTE sponsors student achievement awards for excellence in writing.

Publications

Nine monthly or quarterly professional journals; pamphlets, books, newsletters, and cassettes. Among the journals are *College English,* monthly, aimed at the college scholar and teacher; *English Journal,* monthly, presenting the latest developments in teaching reading at the middle, junior high, and senior high school levels; *Language Arts,* monthly, for elementary school reading and language teachers and teacher trainers; and *SLATE Newsletter,* six times a year, summarizing national news affecting language arts educators, including new programs at the Department of Education (§83).

Sources of Support

Membership dues, sale of publications, conference fees, and federal funds for the ERIC Clearinghouse.

§65 National Council on the Aging, Inc. (NCOA)

600 Maryland Avenue, S.W., West Wing 100
Washington, D.C. 20024
202-479-1200
800-424-9046
Bella Jacobs, *Project Director, LEEP*
Ronald Manheimer, *Director, SCHP*
Established in 1950

What/For Whom

NCOA is a private, nonprofit organization that serves as a major resource for information, training, technical assistance, advocacy, publication, and research on every aspect of aging. Individual members range from senior center professionals, health care practitioners, and other service providers to gerontologists, agency board members, and personnel directors. Organizational members include adult day care centers, senior housing facilities, senior centers, older worker employment services, and local, state, and national organizations and companies serving the aging.

Examples

1) Literacy Education for the Elderly Project (LEEP). Begun in 1984, this national program offers reading instruction to older adults and trains them as tutors. Supported by a grant from the Fund for the Improvement of Postsecondary Education (FIPSE), an agency of the U.S. Department of Education (§83), the program links the resources of community-based organizations already serving large numbers of older people and the local affiliates of national adult literacy organizations (for example, Laubach Literacy Action [§52] or Literacy Volunteers of America [§54]). A distinctive feature of the program is that older volunteers serve as reading instructors for the older adults who receive the tutoring.

2) Senior Center Humanities Program (SCHP). SCHP is a reading-centered, community discussion program for older adults that focuses on the humanities. The program is intended to expand and diversify the offerings of senior centers, nursing homes, day care centers, nutrition sites, retirement complexes, and other organizations serving older people. Begun in 1976, the program is supported by a grant from the General Programs Division of the National Endowment for the Humanities (§67). Additional funding comes from participating senior centers and sponsoring agencies, and from corporations and foundations. The quarterly newsletter *Collage* is sent to SCHP-participating sites and to others involved in humanities and arts programs for older adults.

3) Educational Goals Inventory (EGI). EGI is a computer-assisted method for setting educational goals that is used by

organizations serving older adults. Senior centers, nursing homes, churches, libraries, and housing centers use the inventory, which was developed by the Educational Testing Service of Princeton, New Jersey, to help them plan and improve educational programs for senior citizens. For example, the inventory could help libraries figure out how to reach older adults in the community; how to work with other community organizations, such as senior citizen centers, in reaching older adults; or how to assess the quality of education programs being offered to older adults. The EGI grew out of a two-year project, "Nontraditional Educational Programs for the Elderly," supported by FIPSE.

Publications

The bimonthly magazine *Perspective on Aging* examines issues, research, and programs on aging. The quarterly annotated bibliography *Current Literature on Aging* lists the most recent books, articles, and periodicals on gerontology.

Sources of Support

Grants from the federal government and from foundations; membership dues; contributions from participating organizations; sale of program guidebooks, software computer programs, and publications; conferences.

§66   National Endowment for the Arts (NEA)

Old Post Office
1100 Pennsylvania Avenue, N.W.
Washington, D.C. 20506
202-682-5451
Mary MacArthur, *Assistant Director, Literature Program*
Established in 1965

What/For Whom

NEA is an independent federal agency established to preserve the nation's cultural heritage and promote the arts. These aims are accomplished through fellowships awarded to individuals of exceptional artistic talent and grants awarded to nonprofit cultural organizations representing the highest quality in such fields as architecture, crafts, education, dance, folk arts, literature, media, museums, music, theater, and the visual arts.

Examples

1) Fellowships for creative writers in fiction, poetry, and other creative prose.

2) Literary publishing. Small Press Assistance grants support noncommercial literary small presses and university and college presses that publish contemporary creative literature of high quality.

3) Audience development. One program, Residencies for Writers, funds residencies, lasting between one week and one year, for published writers of poetry, fiction, creative essays, and other creative prose. NEA is especially interested in projects that support public readings outside large urban centers and in communities traditionally underserved. Cultural organizations at which residencies are located include state arts agencies, colleges, universities, libraries, museums, art centers, radio and television stations, and other professional and community organizations. The program is designed to develop audiences for contemporary writers both in their own communities and in other parts of the country.

Another kind of audience development grant supports such projects as regional small press book fairs, principally outside large urban areas.

4) Writer's Choice Project. In this project, initiated by NEA but now administered by the Pushcart Press, outstanding writers choose the best literary titles published by small presses in the preceding year. Pushcart Press then runs advertisements for the books in the *New York Times Book Review,* the *Los Angeles Times Book Review,* the *Bloomsbury Review, Publishers Weekly, Library Journal,* and *Booklist* (see §13). NEA remains the sole funder for the project. For further information contact Bill Henderson, Pushcart Press, P.O. Box 380, Wainscott, New York 11975, 516-324-9800.

5) PEN Syndicated Fiction Project. The project is a cooperative effort of the PEN American Center (§72), a major writer's service organization, and the Literature Program of the NEA. Judges from PEN select short stories from those submitted in a national competition, and the endowment offers them free at the rate of eight per month to fifteen newspapers for national syndication. The newspapers, which have a combined circulation of 12 million, can pick the stories best suited to their readership, but they must print at least two a month. Authors whose stories are selected receive money from the endowment and additional funds from each newspaper that prints them. For further information contact Richard Harteis, Director, PEN Syndicated Fiction Project, P.O. Box 6303, Washington, D.C. 20015; 301-229-0933.

Publications

The Arts Review is NEA's quarterly review of developments in the arts and progress on endowment-supported projects. In addition, NEA publishes grant application information, available from specific discipline programs.

Source of Support

Federal government.

§67 National Endowment for the Humanities (NEH)

Old Post Office
1100 Pennsylvania Avenue, N.W.
Washington, D.C. 20506
202-786-0271
Thomas C. Phelps, *Program Officer, Division of General Programs*
Established in 1965

What/For Whom

NEH is an independent federal agency established to promote the humanities through grants to humanities projects and scholars in defined areas of humanistic study. These areas include, but are not limited to, "languages, both modern and classical; linguistics; literature; history, jurisprudence; philosophy; archaeology; comparative religion; ethics; the history, criticism, and theory of the arts; those aspects of the social sciences which have humanistic content and employ humanistic methods; and the study and application of the humanities to the human environment with particular attention to the relevance of the humanities to the current conditions of national life." Grants are made through five divisions: Education Programs, Fellowships and Seminars, General Programs, Research Programs, and State Programs; and two offices: the Office of Challenge Grants and the Office of Preservation.

Examples

1) The Office of Preservation provides national leadership and grant support for the preservation of deteriorating books and other paper documents in libraries, archives, museums, historical organizations, and other repositories. Contact Harold C. Cannon, director, 202-786-0254.

2) The Division of Fellowships and Seminars supports scholars, teachers, and others undertaking independent research.

3) The Division of General Programs has several relevant programs:

a. Humanities Projects in Libraries. These are programs through which all types of libraries serving adults—public, community college, university, and special—enhance their communities' appreciation and knowledge of the humanities. Another goal is to increase the appreciation and use of library collections.

A Humanities Projects in Libraries grant is funding the American Library Association's three-year "Let's Talk About It" project (see §13), which involves reading and discussion programs that take place in libraries and explore contemporary themes.

b. Humanities Projects in Media. Projects involve the planning, scripting, or production of television, radio, or film

89

programs in the humanities intended for national distribution and general audiences. Of special interest are programming for children and programs that dramatize or examine classic works of fiction and nonfiction for television and radio.

c. Senior Center Humanities Program (SCHP). SCHP is a reading-centered, humanities discussion program for older adults that is offered at local community sites by the National Council on the Aging, Inc. (see §65), with the help of an NEH grant.

4) The Division of Research Programs has programs of interest as well:

a. Reference Works Program. The program funds the preparation of reference works that will result in the advancement of research and learning in the humanities among professionals and the general public.

b. Subsidies to scholarly publishers. NEH gives grants to university and private presses for publication of books on humanities topics that they would not otherwise be able to publish.

5) Division of State Programs. The division supports humanities programs in individual states. Grants are awarded through a network of humanities councils.

Publications
The magazine *Humanities* is the endowment's bimonthly review of current work and thought in the humanities. It also describes recent grants and progress on projects supported by endowment funding. In addition, NEH publishes grant application information and a variety of special publications.

Source of Support
Federal government.

§68 National Information Standards Organization (Z39)

National Bureau of Standards
Building 101, Room E-106
Gaithersburg, Maryland 20899
301-921-3241
Patricia Harris, *Executive Director*
Established in 1939

What/For Whom
The National Information Standards Organization (Z39) develops and promotes standards for electronic and paper information systems, products, and services, including libraries and publishers. Z39's sixty members include libraries; profes-

sional, technical, and educational associations; abstracting and indexing services; publishers; government agencies; and commercial and industrial organizations. Z39 participates in the International Organization for Standardization (ISO). About twenty projects are in progress; some involve the development of entirely new standards, others are for the revision of older ones.

Examples

1) The international standard book number, ISBN, and international standard serial number, ISSN, which facilitate the handling of books and periodicals at all levels of distribution, were defined by Z39 standards.

2) Z39 has defined paper quality for library books and is now preparing standards for the storage of archival materials.

3) Z39 is developing a number of standards that will allow computer-to-computer transmission of invoices for book purchasing, the exchange of bibliographic information, and updates of information on in-print titles.

4) Z39 has developed various order forms and defined the elements to be included in other forms.

Publications

About forty-five reports of standards are in print. A quarterly, *Voice of Z39,* provides ongoing information about Z39 activities.

Source of Support

Membership fees.

§69 National PTA

700 North Rush Street
Chicago, Illinois 60611-2571
312-787-0977
Tari Marshall, *Director of Public Relations*
Established in 1897

What/For Whom

The National PTA is a volunteer association that seeks to unite home, school, and community in promoting the education, health, and safety of children. Working through national, state, and local PTA associations, the organization has been active in child advocacy causes. These include securing child labor laws; supporting compulsory public education, including kindergarten; creating a national public health service and developing health, safety, and nutrition programs for children; promoting education for children with special needs; providing parenthood education; organizing and improving school libraries; and establishing a juvenile justice system. The association is also concerned with the issue of adequate funding for public education. Most PTA members are parents, but some are teachers, school administrators, students, senior citizens, and individuals with or without children.

91

Examples	The PTA emphasizes the role of both parents and teachers in helping children learn to read and take pleasure in reading. In 1981, the National PTA, along with the International Reading Association (§51) and two other organizations, sponsored a symposium on "Reading and Successful Living" under the auspices of the Center for the Book in the Library of Congress. Although the national association has no current reading program, many local chapters sponsor reading programs.
Publications	The association's magazine, *PTA Today,* published seven times a year; the newsletter *What's Happening in Washington,* which keeps PTA members informed about pending federal legislation affecting children and youth; brochures on evaluating schools, juvenile justice systems, television, preschool development, and other subjects; and *Looking in on Your School: A Workbook for Improving Public Education,* a guide for parents and others interested in evaluating and strengthening their schools.
Sources of Support	Membership dues; sale of publications; proceeds from conventions; foundation assistance.

§70   O.P.A.M. America, Inc.

1325 Otis Street, N.E.
Washington, D.C. 20017
202-832-6348
Fr. John Bertello
O.P.A.M. founded in 1973; O.P.A.M. America established in 1985

What/For Whom	O.P.A.M. America is the U.S. branch of the international literacy promotion organization O.P.A.M., for *Opera di Promozione della Alfabetizzazione Mondio* (literally, "Institute for the Promotion of World Literacy"). O.P.A.M. emphasizes functional literacy, aiming, for example, at literacy for farmers selling their produce so they can resist exploitation and at literacy for improving agriculture suitable for local conditions. O.P.A.M. promotes community development in developing countries through centers for literacy, schools of agronomy and crafts, professional technical instruction, domestic science and hygiene schools, and centers for women's development. O.P.A.M. operates by providing resources—money, tools, books, etc.—to groups already operating in the field, mostly missionaries. Founded by Msgr. Carlo Muratore, O.P.A.M. provides support not only to Catholic missionaries, but to Protestant missionaries and others as well. O.P.A.M. America educates Americans about the extent of world illiteracy and its results and raises funds for O.P.A.M.
Example	In 1982, Unesco conferred an honorable mention award on O.P.A.M., "for the efforts realized through many years of educating the public to the nature and dimensions of illiteracy in

the world, and for the moral and material support generously given in the area of education in Africa, Asia, and Latin America."

Source of Support   Contributions.

§71   Paideia Group

Institute for Philosophical Research
101 East Ontario Street
Chicago, Illinois 60611
312-337-4102
John Van Doren, Senior Fellow, Institute for Philosophical Research
Established in 1979

What/For Whom

The Paideia Group is an informal group of twenty-two nationally recognized educators committed to a special agenda for improving the United States education system at all levels, grades K through 12. The group's 1982 manifesto for educational reform calls for a three-part teaching process in which lectures and textbook assignments are only the first step, to be followed by, secondly, coaching, to form the habits through which skills are permanently mastered, and, thirdly, Socratic teaching, a seminar format in which students answer questions and discuss the answers. The proposal is aimed at eliminating the inequities of the two-track system of schooling, which educates college-bound students in one way and those who are not college-bound in another. Paideia's overall purpose, then, is not only to improve the quality of basic schooling in the United States, but also to make that quality accessible to all children, without assumptions about whether they are ultimately "destined for labor" or "destined for leisure and learning."

The Paideia Program does not represent a single specified curriculum to be adopted uniformly throughout the nation, but instead presents a framework within which a variety of curricula can be instituted. It is intended for teachers who wish to apply its recommendations in their schools and classrooms, for school administrators and those involved in the training of teachers, for school board members, and for parents involved in the schooling of their children.

The Paideia Group is headquartered at the Institute for Philosophical Research, which was founded in 1952 by Mortimer J. Adler to explore key philosophical concepts, such as freedom, love, happiness, and progress as they are regarded by the most renowned authors of Western civilization. Adler, Director of the Institute for Philosophical Research and Chairman of the Board of Editors of Encyclopaedia Britannica, is also chairman of the Paideia Group.

Example	Paideia initiatives are being tried at Skyline High School in Oakland, California, the Atlanta Public Schools, two high schools and two elementary schools in Chicago, and various other schools across the country.
Publications	Mortimer J. Adler has written a trilogy that explains the Paideia agenda for educational reform: *The Paideia Proposal* (1982), *Paideia Problems and Possibilities* (1983), and *The Paideia Program* (1984). *The Paideia Program* includes at the end a list of recommended readings arranged by grade level: K through 4, 5 through 9, and 10 through 12.
Source of Support	The Paideia Group is funded through the Institute for Philosophical Research by contributions from corporations and foundations.

§72 PEN American Center

568 Broadway
New York, New York 10012
212-334-1660
John Morrone, *Programs and Publications*
Established in 1921

What/For Whom PEN American Center is the largest of 82 centers that comprise PEN International, a worldwide association of professional writers and the chief voice of the international literary community. The organization promotes friendship and intellectual cooperation between writers within each nation and writers of different nations. Included in PEN International are five centers for writers living in exile.

PEN stands for "poets, playwrights, editors, essayists and novelists"; members also include translators, historians, critics, and biographers. Membership is by invitation. PEN's activities include panel discussions, receptions for authors, conferences, international congresses, and assistance to writers in prison and American writers in need. PEN also gives a number of prizes and awards, including the Ernest Hemingway Foundation Award for first novels, the PEN/Faulkner Award for fiction, and the PEN/West Small Press Publishers Award.

Examples 1) Freedom to Write Program. The program defends freedom of expression in the United States and around the world. Abroad, it works in cooperation with an international network of writers and human rights organizations to monitor possible threats to writers and writing and takes diplomatic and legal action. The domestic component of the Freedom to Write Program is called the American Right to Read Project. It was developed to encourage public discussion of book censorship problems in the communities where they occur. PEN sends writers, covering their expenses, from every discipline and from every region of the country into communities where books are being removed or restricted. The visiting writer can then speak in classrooms, libraries, churches, at PTA meetings, or at other public gatherings. The Freedom to Write Program also serves as a national clearinghouse for information on book censorship; provides American writers with litigation assistance, including amicus curiae briefs and expert testimony; and makes available a one-hour videotape documentary in which well-known writers read from books being banned or challenged in the United States.

2) PEN Syndicated Fiction Project. A cooperative venture of the PEN American Center and the Literature Program of the National Endowment for the Arts (§66), the project promotes the reading of fiction of contemporary American writers by syndicating short stories in newspapers around the country. PEN judges select the short stories in national competition, while the endowment distributes them for syndication and also directly compensates the writers.

Publications

The *PEN Newsletter,* quarterly; the *Freedom-to-Write Bulletin,* irregular; *Grants and Awards Available to American Writers,* a biennial directory; and many reports, pamphlets, and books.

Sources of Support

Sale of publications and videotapes; contributions from individuals, corporations, and foundations; funding from National Endowment for the Arts for the PEN Syndicated Fiction Project.

---

§73 Poets & Writers, Inc.

201 West 54th Street
New York, New York 10019-5564
212-757-1766
Elliot Figman, *Director*
Established in 1970

What/For Whom

Poets & Writers, Inc., is a nonprofit service organization for the United States literary community. It publishes material on practical, writing-related topics, such as copyright, literary agents, literary bookstores, workshop sponsors, grants, and taxes. It helps pay writers' fees for public readings and workshops in New York State and provides assistance to groups wishing to start such programs. It supplies addresses, facts, and referrals of interest to the writing community nationwide.

Examples

1) Readings/Workshops Program. With principal support from the Literature Program of the New York State Council on the Arts and additional private contributions, the program pays fees to writers who give readings or workshops sponsored by groups in New York State. The purpose of the program is to develop audiences for contemporary literature and to help writers survive financially.

95

2) Information Center. The center will supply free of charge, over the telephone, facts or information about the professional side of writers' lives, give writers' current addresses, and answer questions relating to writers' practical needs.

Publications

The newsletter *Coda*, five times a year, provides practical news and comments on publishing, jobs, grants, taxes, and other topics. The organization also publishes references, source books, and guides.

Sources of Support

Grants from the Literature Program of the National Endowment for the Arts (§66), and the Literature Program of the New York State Council on the Arts; contributions from corporations, foundations, and individuals.

§74 Push Literacy Action Now (PLAN)

2311 18th Street, N.W.
Washington, D.C. 20009
202-387-7775
Michael R. Fox, *Executive Director*
Established in 1972

What/For Whom

PLAN is a nonprofit literacy program for adults that serves the community of the District of Columbia and addresses literacy problems on a national scale. Primarily a volunteer organization, it provides tutoring, testing, information and referral services, teacher training, and advocacy. Believing that one-on-one literacy teaching is neither successful nor economically efficient, PLAN emphasizes small-group classes. Instruction is provided to individuals in-house and to local companies in the workplace. The focus is on adults reading below the sixth-grade level.

PLAN's program emphasizes the need for changes in the society that surrounds those who cannot read. PLAN advocates acceptance of new regulations governing the readability of printed matter for the general public and teaches workshops in writing and analyzing welfare and school reports, manuals, legal and insurance documents, and other communications for more widespread readability. PLAN also urges that literacy be regarded as a basic rather than a support service. In order to attract greater numbers of people to literacy instruction in the future, for example, PLAN believes that it will be necessary to provide them with such support services as transportation (to help get them to literacy classes) and child-care services.

Examples	1) Writing for Readability Program. In addition to holding literacy classes in business locations, PLAN also provides readability workshops to help those who write company copy see the need and the way to rewrite materials to meet a sixth-grade reading level.

2) Operation Wordwatch. Wordwatch is a program designed to enhance literacy for marginally literate adults by increasing the readability of public information, which is routinely written at or near a college reading level and often in a highly indirect style. As part of its national literacy initiative, B. Dalton Bookseller has asked PLAN to help with its in-house communications and public marketing materials.

Publication

PLAN's bimonthly newsletter, *The Ladder,* distributed nationally for the last three years, offers incisive, often controversial, reviews of literacy programs and developments.

Sources of Support

Contributions from foundations, community groups, corporations, and individuals; minimal tuition fees paid by students.

---

§75 Reading Is Fundamental, Inc. (RIF)

Smithsonian Institution
600 Maryland Avenue, S.W., Suite 500
Washington, D.C. 20560
202-287-3220
Ruth Graves, *President*
Established in 1966

What/For Whom

Founded by Mrs. Robert McNamara, RIF is a private, nonprofit organization that works through local communities to motivate children (from age three through high school) to read and own books. RIF projects select and buy inexpensive books and offer them to youngsters at "book distributions," festive occasions when young people select and keep books that they like. The national RIF organization has helped start RIF projects in schools, libraries, hospitals, day care centers, correctional facilities, and migrant farmworker communities. The projects are run largely by volunteer citizens and involve parents, educators, members of service clubs, librarians, community leaders, and others.

In addition to book distributions, RIF stages other reading-related activities at the grassroots level throughout the school year and often during the summer, for example, dramatic skits, poster and essay contests, and talks on reading by athletes and entertainers. Recently RIF began providing workshops and publications to teach parents how to encourage their children's reading.

Among RIF's services to local projects are guidance materials and workshops, special discounts and services from book suppliers, information on reading motivation techniques, and a nationwide campaign to promote reading through public service announcements on television and in the print media.

RIF is associated with the Smithsonian Institution; the Chairman of the Board is Mrs. Elliot Richardson.

Examples

1) Reading is Fun Week, April 21–27, 1985, marked RIF's new program, "In Celebration of Reading." Those who satisfied the Celebration's reading requirement at the local level were eligible for a national drawing, the winners of which received a trip to Washington, D.C., for an awards ceremony and a library of paperback books. Funded through a grant from the National Home Library Foundation, the "In Celebration of Reading" program is designed to encourage youngsters to read, outside of school hours, books unconnected with school assignments.

2) RIF benefitted in 1984 from New American Library's pledge of one cent for every copy of a Signet Classic sold during the year.

Publication

RIF Newsletter, quarterly; booklets and instructional pamphlets.

Sources of Support

Contributions from private corporations, foundations, and individuals; federal government support through the Smithsonian Institution.

§76 Reading Rainbow

202 Riverside Drive, Suite 9B
New York, New York 10025
212-666-1800
Gail Miyasaki, *Publicity/Outreach Coordinator*
Introduced in 1983

What/For Whom

Reading Rainbow is a PBS summer television series, first aired in 1983, that is designed to motivate children to read. The productions mark one of the first collaborations of the publishing and television worlds to promote reading by young viewers coast to coast. Hosted by LeVar Burton, who achieved national television prominence in *Roots,* the series has a half-hour magazine format that features an adaptation of a children's book; a field segment that explores places or ideas mentioned in the book; and reviews by children in the studio audience of three books of related interest. Animation, music, and on-location documentary sequences expand each book's theme to encourage young readers to see books as a part of their everyday lives.

The Association for Library Service to Children, a division of the American Library Association (§13), served on the projects's national advisory council with the National PTA (§69), the Association for Supervision and Curriculum Development, and the International Reading Association (§51). The series is co-produced by WNED-TV, the public television station in Buffalo, New York, and Great Plains National Instructional Television Library in Lincoln, Nebraska, in association with Lancit Media Productions Limited in New York.

Example

A 1985 episode featured *Paul Bunyan* in a children's retelling by Steven Kellogg, narrated by Buddy Ebsen. The on-location segment took place in Maine, the legendary birthplace of Paul Bunyan, where the ideas represented by the logger were explored in sequences on forest rangers and reforestation, emphasizing ecology and environmental conservation.

Publications

Reading Rainbow Gazette, a sixteen-page activity magazine that includes games, puzzles, and photographs from the series as well as a complete *Reading Rainbow* booklist; other specially written materials designed to help parents, libraries, and public television stations to encourage children to read when not in school.

Sources of Support

Funding from the Corporation for Public Broadcasting, private corporations, and foundations; sale of publications, such as the *Gazette;* sale of promotional items.

---

§77 Reading Reform Foundation

7054 East Indian School Road
Scottsdale, Arizona 85251
602-946-3567
Bettina Rubicam, *National President*
Established in 1961

What/For Whom

The Reading Reform Foundation is a national, nonprofit organization committed to restoring phonics as the basic method of reading instruction. A national group with state committees, the foundation provides information on phonetics; sponsors an annual conference and workshops; and offers referral services, including a literacy clearinghouse and technical assistance to remedial reading programs. The emphasis is on children of elementary-school age.

Example	The New York Metropolitan Area Chapter sponsors a volunteer program in which teenage volunteers undergo training in the structure of the language, especially phonetics, and then tutor fourth-graders in inner-city schools.
Publications	*The Reading Informer,* a quarterly newsletter; *Literacy Digest,* a directory that is periodically updated; various manuals, videotape cassettes, booklets, and articles.
Sources of Support	Sale of publications; donations; grants from foundations; individual contributions.

§78 Society for Scholarly Publishing (SSP)

2000 Florida Avenue, N.W.
Washington, D.C. 20009
202-328-3555
Alice O'Leary, *Administrator*
Founded in 1979

What/For Whom	The Society for Scholarly Publishing is a national organization serving the scholarly publishing community as a whole. Its membership includes university presses, for-profit scholarly and professional presses, professional associations, museums, reference and database publishers, printers, individuals who work in these areas, librarians, and other information professionals. SSP provides for communication among these professionals, gives educational seminars, and in general helps its members to keep abreast of publishing trends, both technological and managerial/administrative. SSP holds an annual meeting in addition to its seminars.
Example	SSP's seminar, "Marketing Scholarly Publications," has been extremely successful and has been repeated in both New York and San Franscisco. The day-and-a-half seminar covers such topics as planning, marketing online services, and marketing books and journals.
Publications	SSP's *Letter,* published six times a year, carries SSP news, announcements of publications and book reviews, an international calendar of relevant conferences, meetings, and seminars, and other articles. SSP publishes the proceedings of its annual meeting.
Sources of Support	Membership fees; grants from foundations; revenues from meetings and seminars.

§79 Southern Baptist Convention — Home Mission Board

Literacy Missions Ministries
1350 Spring Street, N.W.
Atlanta, Georgia 30367
404-873-4041
Mildred Blankenship, *Director*
Established in 1959

What/For Whom   The Home Mission Board of the Southern Baptist Convention promotes and develops literacy training programs through Southern Baptist churches and associations around the country. Literacy is seen as a mission rather than a social service. The ministries train volunteer tutors to work in adult literacy programs, in programs for school-age children, and in English-as-a-second-language programs.

Publication   *Handbook for Literacy Missions* outlines the ministries' rationale and procedures for teaching reading, writing, and conversational English.

Source of Support   The Southern Baptist Church.

§80 Television Information Office (TIO)

National Association of Broadcasters
745 Fifth Avenue
New York, New York 10151
212-759-6800
Roy Danish, *Director*
Established in 1959

What/For Whom   The Television Information Office of the National Association of Braodcasters promotes the social and cultural aspects of television broadcasting and the educational uses of commercial programming. It is concerned with television's impact on society, for example, in such areas as its treatment of violence, its presentation of women, its influence on children, and media reliability. TIO monitors and anticipates trends in the use of the medium and maintains an education program through national mailings, interviews, and participation in conferences. TIO's research center and library is used by educators, students, government agencies, the press, the clergy, librarians, allied communications professionals, and the general public, as well as broadcasters. TIO also organizes panel discussions for national conferences of educational groups, such as the National Council of Teachers of English (§64). For additional information contract James Poteat, Manager of Research Services.

Publications

Among the research projects TIO has commissioned and the many publications currently available are a series of ongoing national surveys, directed by the Roper Organization, about changing public attitudes toward television. *TV Sets-In-Use,* published three times a year, reports on how educators, librarians, parents, and broadcasters are working to increase television's teaching potential for children and lifelong learners. Other material distributed by TIO throughout the teaching profession focuses on television and children.

TIO provides to broadcasters such publications as *Talking Points,* a series of research papers summarizing information and opinions on such issues as children and television, minorities and television, and TV in election politics; *Voices and Values: Television Stations in the Community,* a book describing the various ways commercial broadcasters respond to community needs; and *Television Looks at Aging,* a book about local and network programming efforts for and about older citizens. Among the services TIO provides to writers and the press are *Tele Leads,* short items about television that can be used in columns or as the basis of longer articles. A list of TIO publications can be obtained by writing to TIO.

Sources of Support

TIO is supported by the three major television networks (ABC, CBS, NBC), individual commercial stations and groups, educational stations, the National Association of Broadcasters, and the Station Representatives Association. Additional funding comes from the sale of publications and audiovisual material.

§81 Unesco Division for Book Promotion and International Exchanges

Unesco
7, Place de Fontenoy
75700 Paris, France
33-1568-1000
C. Zaher, *Director*

What/For Whom

The efforts of Unesco's Division for Book Promotion and International Exchanges are currently aimed at goals set at the 1982 World Congress on Books. The congress, whose theme was "Towards a Reading Society," emphasized national development of publishing and book distribution systems, the creation of a reading environment for all ages at all levels of society, and international publishing cooperation and international book trade. Consequently, the division's priorities include programs to train editors, booksellers, book designers, printers, and other book workers in areas where the book trade is underdeveloped; financial and technical support for nations studying and improving national book policies and book distribution systems; the organization of national reading campaigns; assistance in providing reading materials for new literates; research into national problems in the book world and into the future of the book; and reading promotion for particular groups such as children, disadvantaged groups, rural populations, the family, the handicapped, and the blind. Unesco also maintains regional offices for both promotion and development for Latin America and the Carribean (CERLALC), headquartered in Bogota, Columbia; Africa South of the Sahara (CREPLA), in Yaoundé, Cameroun; and Asia and the Pacific (ACCU), in Tokyo.

Example

Latin American Stories and Legends, the first in a series of children's books, recently published in Spanish and Portuguese, is a product of the Unesco-CERLALC Regional Co-operation Programme for Latin America and the Carribean, is financially supported by the International Fund for the Promotion of Culture, and is the result of a copublishing arrangement with Argentina, Brazil, Colombia, and Venezuela.

Publications

Book Promotion News, quarterly, reports not only on the division's activities but on other Unesco and international book promotion projects, conferences, and seminars; international book fairs; professional associations; recent publications relevant to the book trade; awards and prizes; and important national events. The division also publishes a series of studies on national and international book development. One of these, published in 1984, *The Future of the Book, Part III: New Technologies in Book Distribution: The United States Experience,* was prepared by the Center for the Book in the Library of Congress.

Source of Support

Unesco.

---

§82   U.S. Department of Commerce

Washington, D.C. 20230
202-377-0379
William S. Lofquist, *Industry Specialist,* International Trade Administration—Printing and Publishing

What/For Whom

Four agencies within the Department of Commerce engage in activities of particular interest to the book community.

1) Through its Bureau of the Census and other agencies, the Department of Commerce keeps statistics on United States pub-

lishing and the reading public. The department notes, "The nation's concern with improving reading and educational skills should help the U.S. book industry....As the country's economy shifts toward services and away from goods production, the educational requirements of the workforce take on increased importance." Statistics on newspapers, periodicals, and books trace present and projected developments in the areas of printing, publishing, graphic arts, labor and material costs, advertising, and sales.

2) The International Trade Administration (ITA) was established in January 1980 to promote world trade and to strengthen the international trade and investment position of the United States. Its functions include (a) export promotion—trade exhibits, trade missions, catalog and video displays, and the rental of overseas trade centers, (b) formation of trade policy—including the protection of U.S. intellectual property overseas, and (c) trade analysis—studies of trade barriers, publication of trade data, and preparation of the annual *U.S. Industrial Outlook*, which consists of economic reviews and forecasts on the U.S. book publishing industry.

3) The National Bureau of Standards is concerned primarily with the effective application of science and technology for the benefit of the public. Since 1979, the bureau has funded a program to bring librarians from developing countries to the United States for training in the librarianship of technical, scientific, and professional publications. For additional information, contact the Library Division.

4) The National Technical Information Service (NTIS) is the central source for the public sale and distribution of government-sponsored research, development and engineering reports, foreign technical reports, and reports prepared by local government agencies. Periodicals, data files, computer programs, and U.S. government-owned patent applications are also available. Anyone may search the NTIS Bibliographic Data Base online, using the services of organizations that maintain the database for public use through contractual relationships with NTIS. The agency is self-supporting in that all costs of its products and services are paid from sales income.

During fiscal 1979, NTIS began a concerted effort to increase its foreign technical literature collection and to make it readily available, through translation and other means, to American industry. Funds for English-language translations of foreign technical publications are allocated through the agency's Foreign Technology Utilization Program. Translations of primarily Eastern European technical and scientific publications are supported by funds available to the National Science Foundation through Public Law 480. For additional information, contact the International Technology Exchange.

Publications	*Census of Manufactures, Annual Survey of Manufactures,* and *County Business Patterns,* published on a periodic basis by the Bureau of the Census, contain extensive statistics on U.S. book publishing (statistically classified as industry 2731). The *U.S. Industrial Outlook,* published annually by the International Trade Administration, contains economic analyses and projections on the book publishing industry. Full summaries of current U.S. and foreign research reports are published regularly by NTIS is a wide variety of weekly newsletters, a biweekly journal, an annual index, and various subscription formats.
Source of Support	Federal government.

§83   U.S. Department of Education

400 Maryland Avenue, S.W.
Washington, D.C. 20202
202-245-3192

What/For Whom	The Department of Education establishes policies for, administers, and coordinates most federal assistance to education. The secretary of education advises the president on education plans, policies, and programs of the federal government. The secretary directs department staff in carrying out the approved activities and promotes public understanding of the department's objectives and programs.
	Offices and divisions within the Department of Education that conduct programs of special interest to the book community include: the Adult Literacy Inititative (§84); Bilingual Education; Clearinghouse on Adult Education (§85); Library Programs; Center for Statistics; Information Services; Office of Research (§86); Postsecondary Education; and Vocational and Adult Education.
Examples	1) The Office of Bilingual Education and Minority Languages Affairs works for equal educational opportunity and improved programs for "limited proficiency and minority languages populations" by providing support for programs, activities, and management initiatives that meet their special needs for bilingual education.
	2) The Library Programs unit is responsible for making grants to support public and research libraries. Formed in 1985, this unit (formerly a division) is involved in establishing and improving public library service in areas where it is inadequate or nonexistent (for example, in rural areas, to state-supported institutions, to those who are blind and physically handicapped, to those with limited English-speaking proficiency, and

to the aged). The Library Services and Construction Act also mandates funding for the construction of new library buildings, renovation, and purchase of land to establish and maintain cooperative activities among various types of libraries. Former programs of the Division of Library Programs provided help for library literacy programs for adults and school dropouts and grants to enable public libraries to develop and coordinate library literacy programs, providing for training of librarians and volunteers to carry them out , acquiring of materials, and use of library facilities. For additional information, contact Anne J. Mathews, director of Library Programs, 202-254-5680.

In response to the National Commission on Excellence in Education's report *A Nation at Risk*, the Center for Libraries and Education Improvement in the Office of Educational Research and Improvement in 1983 organized a series of seminars to examine what role the library and information science communities should play in helping to create a "learning society." The result of their deliberation was *Alliance for Excellence: Librarians Respond to "A Nation at Risk."* Another publication from the Center for Libraries and Education Improvement, entitled *The Literacy Challenge: A Report of LSCA Literacy Activities FY 82-FY 84,* includes annotated descriptions of Library Services and Construction Act literacy projects funded by the Division of Library Programs during that time.

3) The Center for Statistics gathers, analyzes, and synthesizes data on the characteristics and performance of American education. The area covered includes public and nonpublic elementary and secondary education; postsecondary education, including college and university libraries; and vocational and adult education. The unit was formed in the fall of 1985 to take over the information-gathering and analysis functions of the predecessor National Center for Education Statistics (NCES). Areas typically surveyed by NCES included programs; staffs (race, sex, and salary); and finances.

4) The Information Services, also resulting from the 1985 reorganization of the department, took over reporting functions, many of which had formerly been performed by the Education Statistical Information Office of NCES. The Information Service aims at providing information, particularly research results, to the public, policymakers, and education practitioners (including members of Congress, state departments of education, other federal agencies, college administrators, educational researchers, and business firms).

5) The Educational Resources Information Center (ERIC), now part of Information Services, is a national information system that collects and disseminates findings of research and development and descriptions of exemplary programs in various education fields. ERIC Clearinghouses are operated under federal contract by education organizations and institutions

around the country. ERIC is a major database center for fugitive information on reading, English, speech, journalism, theater, and related communication fields. The clearinghouses or centers collect, evaluate, abstract, and index hard-to-find educational literature; conduct computer searches; commission studies; and act as resource guides. The information collected is listed in the network's reference publications and indexed in extensive computerized files. Each of the sixteen clearinghouses or centers is responsible for a particular educational area. More than seven hundred educational institutions, roughly one-tenth of them abroad, carry the entire ERIC collection and make it available to the public. The clearinghouses are operated under federal contract with the Department of Education. For two examples, see § 27 and 41.

6) The Office of Postsecondary Education formulates policy and directs and coordinates programs for assistance to postsecondary educational institutions and students. Included are programs of student financial assistance, including Basic Educational Opportunity Grants, Direct Loans to Students in Institutions of Higher Education, the Guaranteed Student Loan Program, and Work-Study. The office has promoted the use of work-study students in literacy programs (see the Adult Literacy Initiative, §84).

7) The Vocational and Adult Education Office in the Division of Adult Education provides grants, contracts, and technical assistance for vocational and technical education, professional development in education, community schools, and comprehensive employment and training. It runs the Clearinghouse on Adult Education (§85). It also funds on a matching basis the Adult Basic Education Program (ABE), one of the largest adult basic skills programs in the nation, launched in 1964. It is administered at the state level by state education agencies and at the local level by school districts and uses paid instructors and some volunteer tutors. The ABE program provides instruction in reading, writing, and other basic skills, including English as a second language. For additional information, contact Paul Delker, director, 202-245-9793.

8) The National Awareness Campaign of the Coalition for Literacy (§36) was launched with funds from the Department of Education and others.

Publications

In addition to the publications of individual ERIC centers, ERIC prepares the reference periodical *Resources in Education* (RIE), a monthly journal containing abstracts of each education item that ERIC collects and makes to current educational periodicals containing ERIC annotations of journal articles.

Source of Support

Federal government.

107

§84

U.S. Department of Education — Adult Literacy Initiative

400 Maryland Avenue, S.W., Room 4145
Washington, D.C. 20202
202-472-9020
Joseph H. Casello, *Deputy Director*
Established in 1983

What/For Whom

The U.S. Department of Education (§83) in 1983 established the Adult Literacy Initiative to work both within the government and outside of it to combat illiteracy among youths and adults who were out of school. The initiative is intended to serve and coordinate federal literacy activities in the Department of Education and other departments and agencies, to encourage state and local literacy initiatives, and to promote corporate and union participation in literacy efforts. It also cooperates with the Coalition for Literacy (§36) and B. Dalton Bookseller in the coalition's National Awareness Campaign against illiteracy. The initiative has no regulatory or grant-making authority; its mission is purely one of advocacy.

Examples

1) Head Start Adult Literacy Activities. Much of the Department of Education's literacy activities focus on the intergenerational effects of illiteracy: the relation between a parent's and a child's level of literacy; the effect of adults on the formation of children's reading habits; the presence or absence of books in the home. The Adult Literacy Initiative and the National Head Start Bureau of the Department of Health and Human Services have collaborated on an intergenerational pilot program, focusing on the parents of Head Start children. Head Start offers preschool programs for economically disadvantaged children, emphasizing major parental involvement.

2) College Work-Study Literacy Projects. The initiative has worked with the Office of Postsecondary Education to promote the involvement of postsecondary schools in literacy activities through student and faculty volunteerism, for-credit practicum courses and the use of college work-study students in literacy programs.

3) Federal Employee Literacy Training Program (FELT). Through the Federal Interagency Committee on Education, the initiative created FELT, which recruits volunteers for local literacy programs from federal agencies in all regions of the country and locates available federal space for use by literacy programs. The initiative has also produced a short videotape on FELT for use by participating agencies in their recruitment efforts.

108

4) By coordinating with the Office of Special Education and Rehabilitative Services within the Department of Education, the Initiative has helped to make literacy services available to youths and adults with learning disabilities.

5) AOIP/Department of Education Task Force. The initiative has helped the Department of Education establish a working relationship with the Assault on Illiteracy Project (§18), an affiliation of over eighty major national black organizations dedicated to mobilizing the black community at the grass roots level on behalf of adult literacy. The initiative's efforts in this area are part of a larger effort to focus attention on special literacy needs through meetings, conferences, and ongoing communication.

6) Intradepartmental Minority Languages Task Force. Through this task force, the initiative will conduct a seminar series on the unique literacy learning needs of minority language populations.

7) The initiative supports exploration of the role of technology in advancing literacy. It encourages partnerships for the development of such new literacy technology as computer software and videodiscs through meetings with computer companies and a recent Literacy Technology Conference.

8) National Adult Literacy Project (NALP). The initiative has worked with the National Institute of Education (§86) on ways to disseminate the findings of the NALP study of promising literacy practices and programs.

Publications   Informational brochures and fliers.

Source of Support   Federal government.

---

§85 U.S. Department of Education— Clearinghouse on Adult Education

ROB 3, Room 5610
400 Maryland Avenue, S.W.
Washington, D.C. 20202
202-245-9793
Paul Delker, *Director,* Division of Adult Education, Office of Vocational and Adult Education
Established in 1974

What/For Whom   The Clearinghouse on Adult Education is part of the U.S. Department of Education (§83). It provides information and referral services in the area of adult education, including literacy and English as a second language. The U.S. Department of Education Adult Literacy Initiative (§84) has served as a catalyst for the clearinghouse's ongoing work.

Publications   *Bibliography of Clearinghouse on Adult Education Resource Materials,* which includes sections on literacy, English as a second language, and "Older Persons"; informational brochures.

Source of Support   Federal government.

---

§86   U.S. Department of Education— Office of Research

400 Maryland Avenue, S.W.
Washington, D.C. 20202
202-254-5710
Established in 1985

What/For Whom   The Office of Research, created in the reorganization of the Department of Education in 1985, took over most of the functions previously performed by the National Institute of Education (NIE), which was created by Congress in 1972 as part of the Department of Health, Education, and Welfare and became part of the Cabinet-level Department of Education when that was created in 1979. Its purpose is to support fundamental research at every institutional level of education on the process of teaching and learning, the content of education, and other key issues.

Examples   1) The Teaching and Learning (T&L) Program focuses on literacy. It supports research in reading, writing, mathematics, reasoning, testing, effective teaching, learning outside school settings, and the educational needs of cultural and linguistic minorities. It examines all aspects of teaching—teacher preparation and development; the recruitment, selection, and evaluation of teachers; the teaching environment; and new approaches to instruction. A special Literacy Team, formed in 1978, coordinates program activities and resources which pertain to literacy research and development.

2) In 1983, NIE funded the National Adult Literacy Project (NALP), a fourteen-month study conducted cooperatively by the Far West Laboratory in San Francisco and The NETWORK in Andover, Massachusetts. NALP goals were to gather, analyze, and disseminate data on model literacy programs around the country, develop new forms of technical assistance to strengthen existing programs and design new ones, and shape a priority research agenda as a basis for future literacy planning

and provision. The findings from the project, now completed, will be available in twelve reports and monographs and a guidebook. For further information, contact Mike Brunner, 202-254-5654.

Publications

In 1985, the NIE released a major report on reading, *Becoming a Nation of Readers,* produced under the auspices of the National Academy of Education. The report is available from the Center for the Study of Reading (§31) and the International Reading Association (§51).

Source of Support

Federal government.

---

§87   U. S. Information Agency (USIA)

400 C Street, S.W.
Washington, D.C. 20547
202-485-2866
Guy Story Brown, *Director,* Cultural Centers and Resources

What/For Whom

The United States Information Agency is responsible for the government's overseas information and cultural programs. Several of its activities are of special concern to the book community, including the USIA library, book export, translation, exhibits, and book donation programs. Several of these programs are reviewed in the Center for the Book publication, *U.S. Books Abroad: Neglected Ambassadors* (1984), by Curtis G. Benjamin. The USIA also encourages person-to-person exchanges that sometimes include publishers, librarians, and booksellers. One such project, sponsored jointly with the Center for the Book, is described in *The International Flow of Information: A Trans-Pacific Perspective* (Library of Congress, 1981).

Examples

1) USIA maintains 130 libraries in 80 countries. Their collections offer a representative selection of current American publications, covering a broad range of areas in the social sciences and the humanities. Some libraries also maintain core collections that highlight classics of American thought and literature. For further information, contact Richard Fitz, chief, Library Program Division, 202-485-2915.

2) The Book Program Division organizes exhibits of American books for major international book fairs. This division also assembles exhibits of appropriate American publications for overseas professional events, seminars, libraries, and scholarly institutions. For further information, contact Jerry Prillaman, chief, Book Program Division, 202-485-2896.

3) USIA promotes translations of American books into Spanish, French, Arabic, Portuguese, and a dozen other languages. USIA promotes and participates in translation projects in a variety of subsidy, co-editing, and copublishing arrangements, often with local publishers in third-world countries.

Source of Support   Federal government.

---

§88   White House Conference on Library and Information Services Taskforce (WHCLIST)

1700 East Las Olas Boulevard, Suite 100
Fort Lauderdale, Florida 33301
305-525-6992
Barbara Cooper, *Chair*
Founded in 1979

What/For Whom   WHCLIST promotes and monitors the implementation of the resolutions of the 1979 White House Conference on Libraries and Information Services. WHCLIST's 118 voting members are elected by the original conference participants. In addition, WHCLIST has Associate Members—organizations, institutions, corporations, businesses, and individuals—who have agreed to assist in achieving the taskforce's objectives and who pay annual membership fees. In general, the 1979 White House conference promoted the value of library and information service as a national resource. It debated and adopted sixty-four resolutions ranging in subject from support for freedom of speech, to access to information, to school libraries, to international information exchange. In support of these resolutions, WHCLIST monitors progress at the national and state levels, testifies at state and congressional hearings on relevant issues, and promotes citizen involvement in friends of libraries groups and other cultural organizations.

Examples   1) WHCLIST annually compiles a *Report from the States* that details progress towards implementation of the White House conference resolutions. A national five-year review was also prepared in 1984 and updated in 1985.

2) WHCLIST sponsors awards every year for the Outstanding Legislator, the Outstanding Citizen, and the Outstanding Publication of the year.

Publications   Annual *Report from the States; LISTEN* (Library and Information Services Educational Newsletter); the five-year review.

Sources of Support   Associate Members' fees; contributions; grants.

§89 Women's National Book Association (WNBA)

160 Fifth Avenue, Room 604
New York, New York 10010
212-675-7804
Sandra K. Paul, *President*
Founded in 1917

What/For Whom

The Women's National Book Association is open to men and women in all occupations allied to the publishing industry. WNBA aims at strengthening the status of women in the book industry, sponsoring studies and educational sessions towards this end. WNBA sponsors awards for women in the book industry and for sellers of children's books. WNBA has active chapters in Boston, Cleveland, Detroit, Los Angeles, Nashville, New York, San Francisco, and Washington/Baltimore.

Examples

1) The Constance Lindsay Skinner Award has been given almost every year since 1940 to a distinguished bookwoman for her extraordinary contribution to the world of books and, through books, to society. This award is now given biennially.

2) In spring 1985, the Washington/Baltimore Chapter held sessions on "The Academic as Author & Audience," "An Overview of Nineteenth Century Decorated Cloth Publishers' Bindings," and "How to Sell a Picture Story."

Publications

The Bookwoman is published three times a year individual chapters publish newsletters, as well.

Sources of Support

Membership fees. Publishing companies may become "sustaining members."

A Few Other Resources

A number of resources are too important to pass by completely but did not fit into our main list of organizations for one reason or another. This section will note a number of publications and organizations that also belong to the community of the book.

Publishing. *Publishers Weekly* (New York: R. R. Bowker Company) is the trade magazine of the U. S. book industry. Its articles deal with all aspects of the book trade, and its advertisements announce publications, advertising plans, printing services, and management services. *Publishers Weekly* has been published since 1872, when it broke off from a preceding publication. Recently, *Small Press* (Bowker) has appeared as a monthly devoted to news and feature articles on the small press book world. Other periodicals, such as *Scholarly Publishing* (Toronto: University of Toronto Press), *Fine Print* (San Francisco), and *Small Press Review* (Paradise, California), treat particular aspects of the small press trade.

Literary Market Place (Bowker) is an annual directory of the book trade that includes publishers; book clubs; literary agents; book distributors; book trade, writers', and press associations; upcoming events such as book fairs and meetings of associations; educational courses for the book trade; literary and book trade awards; consultants; book producers; advertising agencies; translators; direct mail advertising services; book review contacts; wholesalers; book manufacturers; paper suppliers; binders; and more. The same publisher publishes *International Literary Market Place*, which provides similar information on a worldwide scale, and, since 1983, *The Book Publishing Annual*, a review of the year in the book trade.

Broadcasting. The broadcasting industry is becoming increasingly interested in producing programs that encourage reading and increase awareness about problems such as adult illiteracy. Public service announcements, documentaries, and special programs are occasionally broadcast on the major commercial television and radio networks and on public television and radio. The Television Information Office (§80) provides information about this programming, along with the following network offices: ABC Community Relations, 1330 Avenue of the Americas, New York, New York 10019; CBS Educational and Community Services, 51 West 52d Street, New York, New York 10019; and NBC Community Relations, 30 Rockefeller Center, New York, New York 10122. The Corporation for Public Broadcasting, in addition to supporting projects such as Reading Rainbow (§76), has given a grant to WQED/TV in Pittsburgh to develop a major PBS television program and outreach project in the field of adult functional illiteracy. As part of this effort, WQED, 4802 Fifth Avenue, Pittsburgh, Pennsylvania 15213, publishes the *Adult Literacy Newsletter*.

Bookselling. *Publishers Weekly*, again, contains much of interest, while *American Bookseller* (American Booksellers Association, §8) is a basic trade magazine. The *American Book Trade Directory* (Bowker) lists bookstores and book wholesalers. Regional book trade organizations and associations exist in most areas. Many parts of *Literary Market Place* are relevant to the bookselling business as well as to publishing. The antiquarian/rare book trade relies on *AB/Bookman's Weekly* (Clifton, New Jersey). *Rare Books 1983-84: Trends, Collections, Sources* (Bowker), edited by Alice D. Schreyer, provides a recent overview of the rare book world, including purchasing trends; bibliography, educational opportunities, and resources; and directories of associations, auctioneers, appraisers, and dealers.

Libraries. *Library Journal* (Bowker), *American Libraries* (American Library Association, §13), and *Wilson Library Bulletin* (New York: H. W. Wilson Company) are all important sources of news and information for all areas of librarianship. In addition, associations, university departments, and professional publishers publish a great number of journals and newsletters for particular sorts of libraries or particular areas of librarianship. The *ALA Yearbook of Library and Information Services* (American Library Association, §13) provides an annual review of events and of the activities of many library professional groups. The *Bowker Annual of Library and Book Trade Information* (Bowker) summarizes news of the year; indicates important research findings; gives bibliographies of important reference books; provides directory information for library and book trade associations and state officials; and gives a calendar of important upcoming events.

Book collecting. Book collecting clubs around the country sponsor a wide variety of programs, exhibitions, lectures, and publications on book collecting, rare books, fine printing, the graphic arts, and so on. Major clubs include the Grolier Club in New York, founded in 1884, the Club of Odd Volumes in Boston, the Rowfant Club in Cleveland, the Caxton Club in Chicago, the Zamorano Club in Los Angeles, the Roxburghe Club in San Francisco, the Baltimore Bibliophiles, and the Pittsburgh Bibliophiles. Two volumes edited by Jean Peters, *Book Collecting: A Modern Guide* (Bowker, 1977) and *Collectible Books: Some New Paths* (Bowker, 1979), provide a comprehensive introduction to book collecting.

Book culture promotion. Book promotion is a function of government in most countries outside the United States. In several countries, however, there are organizations that rely on a combination of private and governmental support to promote books and reading, like the Center for the Book in the Library of Congress. The oldest is Great Britain's National Book League, founded in 1925, which has its headquarters in London. Others are Australia's National Book Council, located in Carlton; the New Zealand Book Council, in Wellington; the Deutsche Lesegesellschaft, in Mainz, Federal Republic of Germany; and the Fundación Germán Sánchez Ruipérez, in Salamanca, Spain. Two other organizations focus on study of the history of books and their role in society: the Herzog August Bibliothek Wolfenbüttel, in Wolfenbüttel, Federal Republic of Germany; and the Institut d'Étude du Livre in Paris. Unesco also maintains a number of regional book promotion centers (§81).

Index

Information in "Is There a Community of the Book?" and "A Few Other Resources" is indexed to page numbers (p.), whereas information in the main body of organizations is indexed to section numbers (§). Section numbers in **boldface** indicate an entry devoted to that organization.

In addition to a few publications indexed here, almost every organization in the main list publishes a newsletter, which has been noted in the entry for that organization.

118

English language, § 57, 64
  as a second language, § 5, 11, 27, 52, 54, 55,
    58, 79, 83, 85, 86
ERIC, § 83
  Clearinghouse on Languages and
    Linguistics, § 27
  Clearinghouse on Reading and
    Communication Skills, § 41, 64
ESOL. *See* English language as a second
  language
Evans, Luther H., p. 6

Farbstein, Janet, § 1
Farina, Janice M., § 17
Federal Communications Commission, § 2
Federal Employee Literacy Training
  Program, § 84
Federal Trade Commission, § 2
FELT, § 84
Figman, Elliot, § 73
*Final Report: The Adult Performance Level
  Study,* § 3
Fine Print, p. 114
FIPSE, § 65
Fitz, Richard, § 87
Florida Center for the Book, § 30
FOLUSA. *See* Friends of Libraries USA
foreign exchange, impact on international
  book trade, p. 7
Fox, Michael R., § 74
Franklin Book Programs, Inc., pp. 7, 9
Frantz, John C., p. 8
free press; freedom of expression; freedom
  to read. *See* censorship
Freedom to Read Committee, § 20
Freedom to Read Conference, 1953, p. 6
Freedom to Read Foundation, § 13, 42
Friends of Libraries USA, § 43
functional literacy, § 3, 70
Fund for the Improvement of Postsecondary
  Education, § 65
Fundación Germán Sánchez Ruipérez
  (Spain), p. 115

Gannett Foundation, § 54
GBF. *See* Great Books Foundation
Gelfand, Morris A., § 15
Gendlin, Frances, § 21
Gibson, Will, § 7
"Give the Gift of Literacy," § 8
Goldfield, Kady, § 40
Government Advisory Committee on Book
  and Library Programs, pp. 7, 8
*Grants and Awards Available to American
  Writers,* § 72
graphic arts and graphic design, § 12, 56. *See
  also* books, design of
Graves, Ruth, § 75
Gray, Dennis, § 38

Great Books Foundation, § 44
Grolier Club, p. 115
Guild of Book Workers, § 45

Hammer, Jeffrey, § 1
handicapped, services for, § 53
Hans Christian Andersen Medal, § 47
Harris, Patricia, § 68
Harteis, Richard, § 66
Henderson, Bill, § 66
Herzog August Bibliothek Wolfenbüttel
  (Federal Republic of Germany), p. 115
high school equivalency, programs for,
  § 3, 11
high school libraries, § 6, 21
Hightower, Caroline, § 12
Hines, Judith D., § 14
hispanic people, § 16, 18, 62. *See also*
  minorities
history of the book. *See* books, history of
Home Mission Board, Southern Baptist
  Convention, Literacy Missions
  Ministries. *See* Southern Baptist
  Convention
Horner, Douglas E., § 25
humanities, § 9, 13, 38, 40, 44, 65, 66, 67, 87
Humanities, § 67

IBBY. *See* International Board on Books for
  Young People
IBC. *See* International Book Committee
"I'd Rather Be Reading," § 20
IFLA. *See* International Federation of
  Library Associations and Institutions
IIA. *See* Information Industry Association
Illinois Center for the Book, § 30
illiteracy. *See* literacy
illustration, § 45. *See also* books, book arts
immigrants, literacy services for, § 27
Information Industry Association, § 46
Information on Washington, § 46
Informational Media Guaranty Program,
  pp. 7-8
Institut d'Étude du Livre (France), p. 115
Institute of Lifetime Learning, § 6
intellectual freedom, *See* censorship
international
  book lending, § 49
  book programs and activity, pp. 7-9; § 47,
    48, 78, 87
  book trade, § 7, 50, 81, 82, 87
  information exchange, § 81, 87, 88
International Board on Books for Young
  People, § 47
International Book Award, § 48
International Book Committee, § 48
International Book Year, pp. 7, 8
International Federation of Library
  Associations and Institutions, § 48, 49
International Freedom to Publish
  Committee, § 20

119

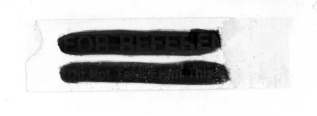